# Sound Steps to Reading

*Foolproof, Scripted Lessons for Reading and Spelling*

## Parent/Teacher Handbook

## Diane McGuinness, Ph.D.

Author: Why Our Children Can't Read

Order this book online at www.trafford.com
or email orders@trafford.com

Most Trafford titles are also available at major online book retailers.

Print information available on the last page.

ISBN: 978-1-4251-8789-7 (sc)

*Trafford rev.  11/25/2019*

www.trafford.com

**North America & international**
toll-free: 1 888 232 4444 (USA & Canada)
fax: 812 355 4082

# Sound Steps to Reading

## Table of Contents

### Section I

### Section II

### Section III

# Section IV

# Section I

## Introduction

## Teaching the Sounds

/p/  /t/  /o/  /m/  /n/  /a/  /d/  /i/  /g/  /b/  /u/  /e/

# Introduction

*Sound Steps to Reading* is revolutionary program based on groundbreaking new research which takes all the guesswork out of how to teach reading and spelling. It is a complete program for teaching beginning readers, suitable for the home or the classroom. General instructions for each of the lessons/tasks are provided below. Detailed instructions for each component are in the lessons themselves. **Please read these instructions carefully.**

### What is a Writing System and How Does it Work?

A writing system is a code for sounds in a language. It works by assigning arbitrary visual symbols to units of speech below the level of the word - marking either syllables, consonant-vowel (CV) combinations, or the consonants and vowels separately. This last type of writing system is known as an "alphabet."

A 5,000 year history of the origin and development of writing systems reveals that no writing system was ever based on the whole word. It is impossible for the average person to memorize more than about 2,000 word symbols even with decades of study. Yet people need around 50,000 words just to carry on a normal conversation. *The Oxford Companion to the English Language* estimates there are around 1,000,000 words in the English language.

**The limits of human memory rule out any type of whole word or 'sight word' reading method.**

Individual consonants and vowels are the *smallest* units of speech that people can hear and are known technically as "**phonemes**." English has 40+ phonemes depending on dialect. Infants rely on their excellent phonemic awareness to learn a language. Over time this skill is lost to conscious awareness as speech becomes automatic. But phoneme awareness is never lost altogether. It can be recovered quite easily IF the child is asked to focus on individual sounds in words. Most four-year-old children can perform routine phoneme awareness tasks quite well. By the same token, a poor reader of any age can recover this skill and learn to read with relative ease. However, unless and until these fundamental skills are made conscious, students won't understand what the letters stand for.

All writing systems are codes, and codes are **reversible** by definition. Sounds in words are first ***encoded*** into symbols and the symbols are ***decoded*** to recover the sounds/words. If there is a perfect correspondence between one sound and one symbol for that sound, alphabetic writing systems are remarkably easy to learn. Unfortunately, the English writing system doesn't play fair. It has multiple spellings for nearly all the sounds in the language. Teaching this complex alphabet code requires knowledge and great care.

**What Children Need to Learn**

Three essential skills are required to guarantee mastery of the English writing system. These are:

> **The ability to hear (discriminate), segment, and blend phonemes in words.**
>
> **The ability to remember which letters or letter patterns stand for which phoneme.**
>
> **The ability to write letter shapes, words, phrases, and sentences fluently and accurately.**

These three skills were found to be essential to reading success in studies carried out in the US and Canada. Researchers made detailed observations of hundreds of individual children during reading lessons at school. They recorded 'time on task' for every activity each child engaged in. The goal was to find out which activities predicted reading skill. The results were identical for all studies. The activities listed above were the *only* positive predictors of reading ability. The more time children spent on these activities, the higher their reading scores were.

By contrast, learning letter names, 'concepts of print' (print direction and turning pages), time spent segmenting syllables, attending to rhyming units in words, and doing 'pretend reading,' or 'group reading,' *had no effect whatsoever*. Some activities produced strongly negative effects, so that time spent on these activities was highly predictive of very poor reading test scores. ***The two most detrimental activities to reading skill were time spent memorizing 'sight words' and listening to the teacher read.***

**The message is clear, if your goal is to teach the English writing system, then teach only the elements that correspond to our alphabet code and no other elements.**

Many European countries like Finland, Sweden, Spain, Italy, Germany, and Austria have a "transparent" alphabet code – one symbol (one spelling) for each of the sounds in the language. Children in these countries learn to read and spell effortlessly in the first year of school. Very few "dyslexic" children can be found in these countries by any definition of the term.

Unfortunately, we do not have a transparent code. Modern written English is a combination of at least four spelling systems superimposed on one another. These have been inherited from the writing systems of the Romans (Latin), Anglo-Saxons, Norman French, and special spellings for words of Greek origin. This confusion is the primary cause of reading and spelling difficulties for a very large proportion of children in English speaking countries around the world.

Here are the major roadblocks for the beginning reader:

1. There are only 26 letters for the 40+ phonemes in our language, not nearly enough. Instead of designing new letters for the left-over sounds, the same letters were reused in pairs: /**sh**/ in 'ship.' These are called '*digraphs*' ('two letters' standing for one sound).

2. Most phonemes can be spelled more than one way. The sound /**ee**/ has 10 spellings, as in : b**e**, s**ee**n, s**ea**t, luck**y**, donk**ey**, s**ei**ze, ch**ie**f, ser**e**n**e**, mar**i**n**e**, rad**i**o.

3. Letters and digraphs can be *decoded* more than one way. The spelling <u>**ou**</u> stands for different sounds in: t**ou**ch, p**ou**nd, s**ou**p, s**ou**l.

It is obvious that this complex code needs to be worked out and then organized in such a way that it can be taught easily and effectively.

There are about 400 different spellings for the 40 sounds in the English language. What we didn't know until recently is which spellings are common and which are not, or how many spellings there are for each sound in the language. In my analysis of these spelling patterns, I identified 176 common spellings that account for about 90% words in print. Once I had this solution, a method was developed to provide a logical and coherent way to teach this complexity so that any child could learn it, and any parent or teacher could teach it.

Because our alphabet code is so complex, it has to be taught the right way around, from sound-to-print. In this way, children can grasp logic and nature of a writing system. This is that the *40 English phonemes are the basis for the code and never change.* These 40 sounds provides a *pivot point* around which the code can reverse, so that reading and spelling can be seen as two sides of the same coin. The 40 sounds will always play fair even if our spelling system does not.

*In Sound Steps to Reading* lessons are designed and ordered in a particular manner so the complexity of the code never becomes an issue. Lessons begin with ***one sound/single-letter*** spellings, followed by ***one sound/two-letter*** spellings (digraphs). Alternative spellings come next (***one sound/more than one spelling***), plus the reverse (***one spelling/more than one sound***).

Every lesson covers all the necessary skills (*and only those skills*) that research has shown are essential: phoneme identification, segmenting, blending, writing, reading, and spelling. The materials are scripted, easy to use, and lessons follow the same sequence throughout - increasing in difficulty only in terms of the spelling code and nothing more.

**No special training is required to use this program**. For the maximum effect, parents and teachers must keep to the lesson sequence and use the scripted text where indicated. Make sure your language is clear and that the following facts are always kept in mind:

**Sounds – not letters - are the basis for our writing system.**

**Sounds are real. Letters are arbitrary symbols (not real).**

**Letters** *stand for* **sounds. Letters do not "have sounds." People do.**

**Avoid using letter names.** Letter names do not stand for the sounds the letters represent and cannot be used to 'sound out' a word. Instead, they are a major source of confusion. For example, the letter names - "*double-you-aitch-ie-el-ee*" ('**while**') -do not remotely represent the three speech sounds in this word: **/w/-/ie/-/l/.**

### The Organization of Sound Steps to Reading

Research on reading has dispelled some cherished myths. One of these myths is that children learn to read by being read to. Think about this in light of what you have just learned. Story-telling goes back to the dawn of history, and stories were only written down fairly recently. Listening to written stories, without any direct instruction in how the code works, will not "teach reading" any more than listening to stories that are just made up as the story-teller goes along. This would be like asking a child to learn musical notation by listening to someone play the piano.

The first innovation in *Sound Steps* is to combine the fun of story-telling with teaching the first basic skill---listening for a sound. Each lesson teaches one of the 40 sounds in our language. The lesson begins with a short portion of a story which features the target sound. The stories are written in rhyme in an entertaining way, and can be enjoyed at two levels, as stories in their own right, or as a listening game.

The story is followed by a concrete listening exercise which insures that the child can identify the position of the target sound anywhere in a word. When this is secure, the child is invited to play the story-listening game by signaling to the teacher each time she hears the target sound. This part of the lesson ends with the presentation of the letter symbol for that sound.

In these two exercises alone, the child quickly comes to understand that words are made up of individual speech sounds, that *letters are assigned to real sounds, and that knowing this makes it easy to decode and spell words.*

A second innovation is the order in which sounds are introduced. The sequence is based on the structure of our language and the nature of the spelling code –always moving from simple to complex. For example, early lessons teach **only the sounds that can be spelled with one letter in any position in a word.** This teaches the logic of 'transitivity'- a sound heard anywhere in the word is the same sound. For example, the sound /**p**/ is spelled **p** whether it comes at the beginning or the end of a word: *pat, tap, pop, top, pot, up*, etc. (This may seem obvious to you, but it isn't to a child.)

The third innovation is that each lesson includes only the sound/symbols taught so far, and lessons are cumulative. Every lesson builds on the one before it. All *Word Lists* include ***only the words with the sounds/spellings taught so far***. If a child has had a long break, parents/teachers can back up to the 'comfort zone' where the child has been successful and move forward from there.

Finally, *Sound Steps to Reading* is comprehensive. There are lessons on handwriting, spelling dictation, plus training in all the necessary skills outlined above. After most lessons, there is the "Really Readiing" section featuring little stories which use only the sounds/spellings taught so far.

Finally, the **Parent/Teacher Storybook** contains the complete version of the stories which introduce each lesson. Always read the whole story later the same day. As the lessons progress many children will soon be able to read these stories on their own.

## How to Teach This Program

*Sound Steps to Reading* is primarily for children in the age range four to seven years. It has been designed to provide the simplest access to the code possible, but children need some preliminary skills to find these lessons enjoyable. They need the attention span, eye-hand coordination, and memory ability of an average 4½ year old to master the following sub-skills without difficulty.

Can hear the individual sounds in words (phoneme identification)

Can hear where each sound comes in a word (phoneme sequence)

Can recognize and can write each letter shape (visual/manual coordination)

Can remember which letter goes with each sound (verbal/visual memory)

Can learn how to push sounds together to make a word (blending)

Can learn how to separate sounds in words (segmenting)

Children vary in developmental rate, and skills do not always proceed together in lock step. Don't push. Remember, the older the child, the faster the lessons will go. Because reading is a learned skill (not a natural developmental controlled by genes) it is never too late to teach someone to read.

### Getting Started

If you want children to be successful, begin with a clear plan and sense of purpose. **"I intend to teach my child (or children) to read and I will start on Monday."** Lessons must come at a consistent pace. Don't try to 'ease' children into reading by going slowly. They easily forget when lessons are spaced too far apart. The optimum rate would be a 30 minute lesson five times a week. If five lessons is too fast or too much for your schedule, drop back to three. Be flexible. If the child is surging ahead and wants to move faster, then move faster. If the child is having trouble with any element of the lesson, take more time with that element. If children can't remember what you taught last time, teach the lesson again.

**For teachers in the classroom, our research has shown that it is optimal to introduce about three sounds per week. Daily lessons are necessary, however, to insure all skills are taught and that the stragglers keep up.**

## Special Instructions

When a **sound is indicated,** as opposed to a letter, it is marked with slashes. The sound **/o/** is the middle sound in **'hot.'** Don't use the letter name. A list of the 40 sounds and their order will be found in the Index. Remember, lessons are cumulative so that every lesson builds on the one before. Keep to this order for maximum success Read the following instructions carefully and refer to them often.

## The Order of the Activities for Each Lesson

### The Sound-Targeting Story

Each sound is introduced by reading a few lines of a story featuring the target sound to the child. (***The complete story is in the Storybook. Be sure to read the whole story later in the day.***) Clarify any issues about story content and vocabulary. Proceed with the lesson sequence.

### The Listening Exercise

A structured listening exercise for the target sound follows immediately. Always do this exercise. Follow the script and use only the *sound* that is featured, ***not its letter name.*** If a child has trouble here, add more words and continue the practice. At the end of each listening exercise, go back to the story fragment once more.

### The Story Listening Game.

Read the short version of the story again. This time instruct the child to listen for the target sound. Try to emphasize the target sound by making it a little louder and by *slowing down your reading speed.* Have children signal each time they hear the target sound by raising a finger.

Be flexible. Not even adults will notice the target sound in every word. Once children get the knack of listening for a target sound, signaling isn't as important. – though you should check from time to time that children can do this task.

When you read the complete story, at a later time, make sure the story matches the lesson you have just been teaching, or a previous story, so the story time reinforces what you have taught so far. **Warning**: Parents - Don't read the child's favorite story over and over again. Make a bargain instead. The child gets the favorite story **if** he listens to the story you choose.

**The Target Letter.**

After the Story Listening game *show* the letter symbol for the target sound. This appears on the handwriting page. *Do not refer to it by its letter name*. The goal is to instill an automatic connection between a sound and a symbol. You will need wide-lined paper for this exercise. Teachers should make copies of the handwriting page for each student.

**Warning: Don't begin a lesson unless you have set aside enough time to teach the letter. The listening and writing activities must be connected.**

Begin the handwriting exercise by orienting the child to Left and Right. If necessary, **mark 'left' with a colored paper clip at the top left of the page**. Talk the child through the features of the letter symbol. Point out whether curved lines go away from the paper clip (to the right) or towards it (to the left). Point out whether lines are straight, curved, or at an angle, and if they are tall (well above the line) or hang down (below the line).

Start the exercise by asking children to trace around the letter with their finger, and let them do this several times while they say ***the sound*** the letter stands for (*not the letter name*). Help if necessary.

**Write It, Say It.**

When the child is familiar with the letter, she can begin the writing exercise. Copying letters is critical. This forces the child to *really look* at each feature in the letter to be able to tell them apart. Have the child say the sound as she writes the letters, so that sound and symbol get associated in memory. This activity must always involve *looking* (visual memory), *saying* (speaking/auditory memory), and *writing* (kinesthetic memory) which will get coded together by the brain. This will speed up learning and lead to fluent reading and writing.

Even if children can already write the letters, **do not skip this exercise.** Being able to *say each sound* while it is being written is a critical skill.

Some children may need more help. Here is what the child needs to be able to do.

*Writing Mechanics*

If a child is writing for the first time, have him practice a pencil grip first by tracing pictures, drawing on scratch paper, and copying his name. Use a short, number 2 pencil. The thumb and second finger grip the pencil, and the first finger steadies it from the top. The heel of the hand should rest comfortably on the table. This is the point of balance. Never let a child write with his whole hand off the paper. Motor patterns quickly become habits, so get this right at the beginning.

Our writing system goes from left to right. This applies to the words, to the letters in the words, and often to the individual strokes in each letter. Left-handers will have trouble because their hand covers up what they have just written. 'Lefties' solve this problem by writing with their hand either below the line or above it (hooked posture). Either posture is OK, but it should be consistent.

*Tracing and Writing Letter Shapes*

For the "Write It, Say It" exercise, you will need wide-lined paper and a short, medium-soft pencil. Photocopy the hand-writing page, or copy the letter form to wide-lined paper. The child can directly trace what you have written, and reproduce this on the line below. If necessary, guide the child's hand. Children should copy the letter many times so this becomes easy and writing is fluent. Insure that all strokes go in the right order and direction. Now hand out a blank piece of lined paper and see if the child can write the letter from memory. Be critical. Make sure the letter stands or sits on the line as it is supposed to. Children should **say the sound out loud as they write the letter.**

**Word Fun**

After the first three sounds/letters introduced, a '*Word Fun*' exercise appears. Word Fun is a list of all the words that can be spelled with the sounds learned so far. Words are set out in two columns. On the left side, the letters are spaced apart. The word appears on the right written in the normal way.

**Children should read the segmented version first, saying each sound separately.** Next, they should read the word on the right, 'blending' the sounds together to produce the whole word. Help by illustrating what to do, then insist the child tries it on his own.

From time to time, a few "**special words**" appear at the bottom of the Word Fun page. These 'special words' are either common function words with strange spellings (**the**, **one**) or spellings that haven't been taught yet. These words introduced to make reading text ('*Really Reading*') sound more like standard English.

When the Word Fun exercise is completed, turn it into a writing exercise. Have children **copy** each word onto lined paper, and then **write from memory (spell)** as you dictate some of the words. They must the sound out loud as each letter is being written. The goals for copying are: reproducing correct letter shape, reproducing the correct order of strokes, correct positioning of each letter on the line, equal spacing of letters in a word.

**If a child is weak at these skills, have him practice by writing over the top of a row of letters made by you, use tracing paper to do this. Never skip the writing component of a lesson. This will double the learning rate.**

### Really Reading

Little 'Readers' appear when there are enough Word Fun words to create phrases, sentences, or stories. Children should read these in the normal way. Fluency is the goal here. If a child stumbles on a word, **don't provide the word**. Make her 'sound it out,' by segmenting each sound, then blending the sounds to make the word. Children need to learn that the code is consistent and that they can rely on it. If necessary, help children segment and blend the sounds, then make them do it alone.

**Really Reading is cumulative**. Only the words that have been taught so far are included in the stories. If a child is having trouble, either because you're moving too fast, or because he had too long a break, back up to an earlier, simpler lesson (the comfort zone) and move forward from there. The golden rule is to move ahead *just beyond* the child's competence.

**The Sound Steps Storybook. The complete story to accompany each lesson can be found in the Storybook.** The stories feature the target sound and are written in rhyme, something young children love. Be sure *you read the complete matching story after each lesson ends*, preferably later the same day. You can read the story at snack time, before a nap, or at bedtime, or whenever the child asks. [Note: Children will be able read all the stories with ease when lessons are completed, and often well before.]

**A word of caution. Don't skip over any part of the lesson because you think your child 'knows it already.' Chances are he/she will be using the wrong logic.** Begin at the beginning and simply go faster. If a child complains and says "I already can do this," then say: "Good. Then we can go much faster." If a child has good listening skills, you can skip the story listening game unless he/she wants to do it. Never omit the Listening Exercise or the writing components of the lesson. Writing is critical for assisting visual memory in learning to spell.

To follow up these issues in more depth or to read about the research that underpins *Sounds Steps to Reading*, you can find this information in the following books. The US and UK versions of *Why Our Children Can't Read* have different content relevant to teaching approaches and current practice.

McGuinness, D. (1997). *Why Our Children Can't Read.* Free Press.
    Paperback (1999). Simon and Schuster  (US version)

McGuinness, D. (1998). *Why Children Can't Read.* Penguin Press (UK version)

McGuinness, D. (2004). *Early Reading Instruction.* MIT Press.

## the sound /p/           Poppy Pig

Read the story for enjoyment.  Do the listening exercise.  Then read the story again and ask the child to listen for the sound /p/ - and signal each time he hears the sound /p/.     (Read Instructions, page 9).  Be sure to read the whole story later when the lesson is over.

Pretty Penny is happy
She has a pig named Poppy

Poppy is a pet
The best pet yet

Most pigs are dirty and sloppy
Not Poppy

Poppy is perfectly pink and pale
From the top of her head to the tip of her tail

---

### Listening for the Sound /p/

**Read each sentence below to the child.**

The sound you hear the most in this story is /**p**/.  [Don't say 'pee' or 'puh.'  Say /**p**/ a puff of air.]

Watch my mouth when I say this sound: /**p/.**  Now you say the sound  /**p**/

Say the word '**pig**' and listen for the sound /**p/.**  /**p/** is the first sound in '**pig**'

Say the word '**pop**' and listen for the sound /**p/.**  The sound /**p/** is the first sound and the last sound.  How many /**p/** sounds do you hear in the word **pop**?   [If there is a mistake say what it is, then repeat the word more slowly.]

Say the word   **poppy**  and listen for the sound /**p/.**   How many /**p/** sounds do you hear in  **poppy** ?    [There are two not three.]

When I say the word **poppy** hold up your hand when you hear the sound /**p/.**  I'm going to say each sound slowly.  [Segment the sounds as shown].

        **p—o—pp—y**

Now I'm going to push the sounds together.  Listen for the two /**p/** sounds in **poppy**
-----------------------------------------------------------------------------------------
If the child needs extra practice, do more words with /p/.  When the child has mastered this, reread the story and play the "listening game."   Then do the '**Write It, Say It'** exercise.

14

# Write It, Say It

Before starting this exercise, **review the instructions** on page 11.  The child should trace the large letter with his finger, saying the sound out loud.  Next, have him copy each letter on the line below.  Always use lower case and make sure the rounded part of the **p** sits on the line, and the tail goes below the line.

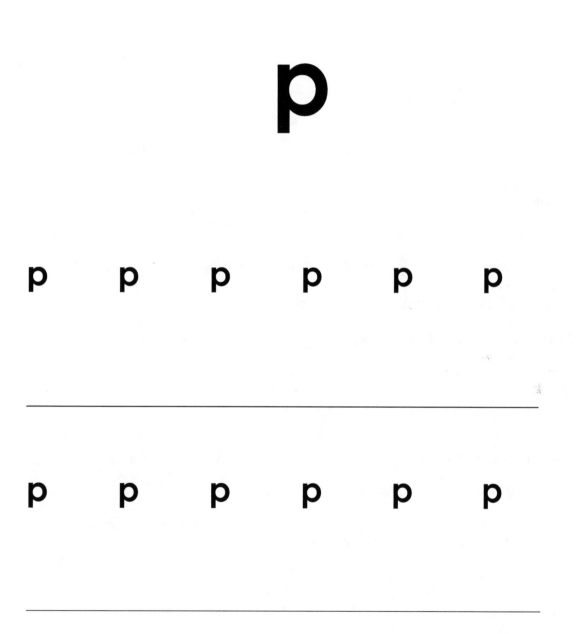

**Have the child practice writing this letter on a separate piece of wide-lined paper, saying the sound as he writes.**

## the sound /t/        Timmy's Terrible Trouble

Read the story for enjoyment.  Do the listening exercise. Then read the story again and ask the child to listen for the sound /t/ - and signal each time he hears the sound /t/.
Be sure to read the whole story after the lesson is over.

This is the tale of Timmy Tuttle.
He lived in the town of Trent-on-Toot
Timmy was smart and quite cute,
but he started to get into terrible trouble
the day that he turned two.

Timmy was a terrific talker.
But now all he said to his mom and his sister was:
    "No!"
    "Don't!"
    "I can't!"
    "I won't!

---

### Listening for the Sound /t/

**Read each sentence below to the child.**

The sound you hear the most in this story is /t/.  [Say /t/ and a puff of air]

Watch my mouth when I say this sound: /t/.  Now you say the sound /t/

Say the word **Timmy** and listen for the sound /t/.   Is /t/ is the first or the last sound in **Timmy.**

Say the word **cat** and listen for the sound /t/.  Is /t/ the first of the last sound?

How many /t/ sounds do you hear in '**toot**'?

When I say the word '**toot**' raise your hand when you hear the sound /t/.  Listen carefully.  I'm going to say each sound slowly.

    **t---oo---t**

Now I'm going to push the sounds together.  Listen for the two /t/ sounds.

    '**toot**'

-----------------------------------------------------------------------------------------
If the child needs extra practice, do more words with /t/.  When the child has mastered this, reread the story and play the listening game.  Then do the "**Write It, Say It**" exercise.

16

# Write It, Say It

The child should trace the large letter with his finger, saying the sound out loud.  Next, have him copy each letter on the line below.   Always use lower case and be sure the t stands on the line.

t     t     t     t     t     t

_____

t     t     t     t     t     t

_____

**Have the child practice writing this letter on a separate piece of wide-lined paper, saying the sound as he writes.**

**the sound /o/     Oliver Talks to the Lochness Monster**

Read the story for enjoyment.  Do the listening exercise.  Read the story again and ask the child to listen for the sound /o/ ('hot').  Be careful, the sound /o/ has alternative spellings (**a** in *a*ll and w*a*ter, **ough** in 'th*ough*t' **aw** in 's*aw*' ).  Play the listening game by having the child signal each time she hears the sound /o/.  Read the whole story after the lesson is over.

Oliver and his dog were sitting on a dock,
on a very large lake called a 'loch.'
People said it was the home of the Lochness Monster.
It lived somewhere underneath the w*a*ter

The problem with this monster
was that it was *a*lways gone.
If you thought you s*aw* it,
it was not for very long.
There were lots of pictures of this monster
but *a*ll of them looked wrong.

---

**Listening for the Sound /o/**

**Read each sentence below to the child.**

The sound you hear the most in this story is /**o**/  [Don't say the letter name.  It's the wrong sound.]

Watch my mouth when I say this sound: /**o**/.  Now you say the sound /**o**/.

Say the word '**on**' and listen for the sound /**o**/.  /**o**/ is the first sound in '**on**'.

Say the word '**fog**' and listen for the sound /**o**/.  /**o**/ comes in the middle of the word.

I'm going to say each sound in the word '**fog**' slowly.  Raise your hand when you hear the sound /**o**/.

    **f ---- o ---- g**

Now I'm going to push the sounds together.  Listen for the sound /**o**/.

    **fog**

---

If the child needs extra practice, do more words with /**o**/.  When the child has mastered this, reread the story and play the "listening game."  Then do the "**Write It, Say It**" exercise for the sound /**o**/.

## Write It, Say It

Have the child should trace the large letter with his finger, saying the sound out loud, then copy each letter on the line below. Use lower case, and be sure the letter **o** sits on the line.

o     o     o     o     o     o

_____

o     o     o     o     o     o

_____

**Have the child practice writing this letter on a separate piece of wide-lined paper, saying the sound as he writes.**

# Word Fun

**Have the child say the sounds these letters stand for (not the letter names).**

# p      t      o

In this exercise, children discover that what they have learned so far can be used to create real words.   The child should read the segmented word in the left column first – saying each sound separately.  Next, they must push the sounds together– as shown in the right column – to create the word.   Model this, if necessary.

| | |
|---|---|
| p—o—p | **pop** |
| t—-o---t | **tot** |
| p---o---t | **pot** |
| t---o---p | **top** |

**top   pot**

Children should copy each word on a piece of lined paper several times.  After this, dictate each word (in a different order) and ask the child to write from memory, sounding out aloud as they write.  **Never omit this part of the lesson**.  It is very important.

## the sound /m/     Mr. and Mrs. Mouse Move House

Read the story for enjoyment.  Do the listening exercise.  Read the story again and ask the child to listen for the sound **/m/** [Extend it—'mmmm'] and signal each time he hears the sound **/m/.** Read the whole story after the lesson is over.

Mr. and Mrs. Mouse and their family
lived in a meadow that was marshy and misty.
Their underground house got damp when it rained,
and Millicent Mouse always complained.

One day, Millicent said to her family,
"This is too much!  We're moving to the city."
So in the middle of the night on a Monday,
ten little mice marched down the highway.

---

### Listening for the Sound /m/

**Read each sentence to your child.**

The sound you hear the most in this story is **/m/**.  [Extend it 'mmmm']

Watch my mouth when I say this sound:  **/m/.**  Now you say the sound **/m/**

Say the word  '**mouse**' and listen for the sound **/m/.  /m/** is the first sound in '**mouse**'.

Say the word  '**home**'  and listen for the sound **/m/.**

Does the sound **/m/** come first or last?  Listen carefully.     I'm going to say the word slowly.  Raise your hand when you hear the sound **/m/.**

       **h---oe---m**

Now I'm going to push the sounds together.  Listen for the sound **/m/.**

       **home**

-------------------------------------------------------------------------------------------------

If a child needs extra practice, do more words with **/m/**.  When the child has mastered this, reread the story and play the listening game.  Then do the "Write It, Say It" exercise for the sound **/m/.**

# Write It, Say It

Have the child should trace the large letter with his finger, saying the sound out loud, then copy each letter on the line below.   Always use lower case, and be sure the letter **m** sits on the line.

m m m m m m

_____

m m m m m m

_____

**Have the child practice writing this letter on a separate piece of wide-lined paper, sounding out as she writes.**

## the sound /n/     Ned Learns How to Be Nice

Read the story for enjoyment. Do the listening exercise. Then read the story again and ask the child to listen for the sound /n/ [Extend it—'nnnn']. Have the child signal each time she hears the sound /n/. Read the whole story after the lesson is over.

Ned is nine and so is Nancy his twin.
They aren't at all alike. How shall I begin?

When Nancy is nice, Ned is naughty.
When Nancy is kind, Ned is mean.
When Nancy is neat, Ned is not.
None of the neighbors want him in.

John and Dan don't like him,
Nor do the others - - none.
They say, "You're noisy and nasty
And not a lot of fun."

---

## Listening for the Sound /n/

**Read each sentence to your child.**

The sound you hear the most in this story is /**n**/ [Extend it 'nnnn']

Watch my mouth when I say this sound: /**n**/.   Now you say the sound /**n**/.

Say the word '**on**'. Say it again and listen for the sound /**n**/ in '**on**'? Is it the first sound or the last sound?

Say the word '**nice**' and listen for the sound /**n**/.   Is it the first sound or the last sound?

How many /**n**/ sounds do you hear in **nine**? I'm going to say this word slowly. Put up your hand when you hear the sound /**n**/

**n---ie---n**

Now I'm going to push the sounds together. Listen for the two /**n**/ sounds in the word:

**nine**

------------------------------------------------------------------------------------
If the child needs extra practice, do more words with /**n**/. Reread the story and play the listening game. Do the "Write It, Say It" exercise for the sound /**n**/.

# Write It, Say It

Have the child should trace the large letter with his finger, saying the sound out loud, then copy each letter on the line below.  Always use lower case, and be sure the **n** sits on the line.

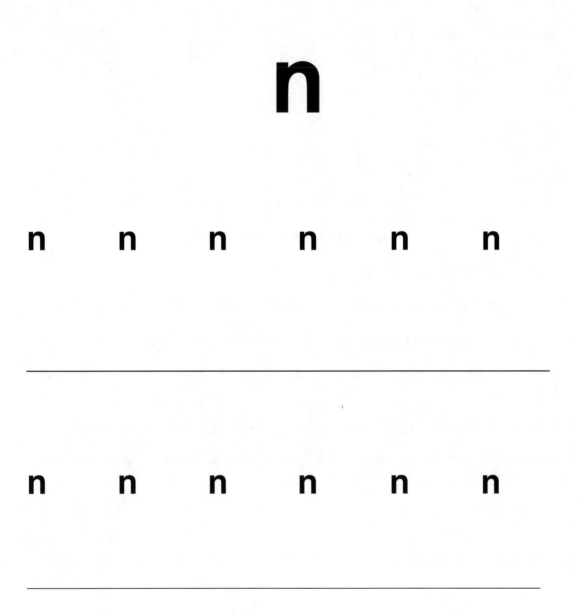

**Have the child practice writing this letter on a separate piece of wide-lined paper, saying the sound as he writes.**

**the sound /a/**　　　　　**Ann's Hat**

Read the story for enjoyment. Do the listening exercise. Then read the story again and ask the child to listen for the sound /a/. Have the child signal each time she hears the sound /a/. Read the whole story after the lesson is over.

Ann had a hat
It wasn't a cap.
It was bigger than that,
more like a bag or a sack
tied on with a strap.

Ann had on that hat
if it was dry or damp.
When she sat in the sand,
she never got tanned,
because she had on that hat.

---

## Listening for the sound /a/

**Read each sentence to your child.**

The sound you hear the most in this story is /**a**/ [Don't say the letter name. It's the wrong sound.]

Watch my mouth when I say this sound: /**a/.** Now you say the sound /**a/.**

Say the word '**Ann**' and listen for the sound /**a/.** Is it the first sound or the last sound?

Listen for the sound /**a/** in the word '**nap**' There are three sounds in the word '**nap**'.

Put up your hand when you hear the sound /**a/.**

　　　**n---a---p**

This time you push the sounds together to make the word.

-------------------------------------------------------------------------------------

If the child needs extra practice, do more words with /**a/.** When the child has mastered this, reread the story and play the listening game. Do the "Write It, Say It" exercise for the sound /**a/.**

# Write It, Say It

Have the child should trace the large letter with his finger, saying the sound out loud, then copy each letter on the line below.   Always use lower case, and be sure the **a** sits on the line.

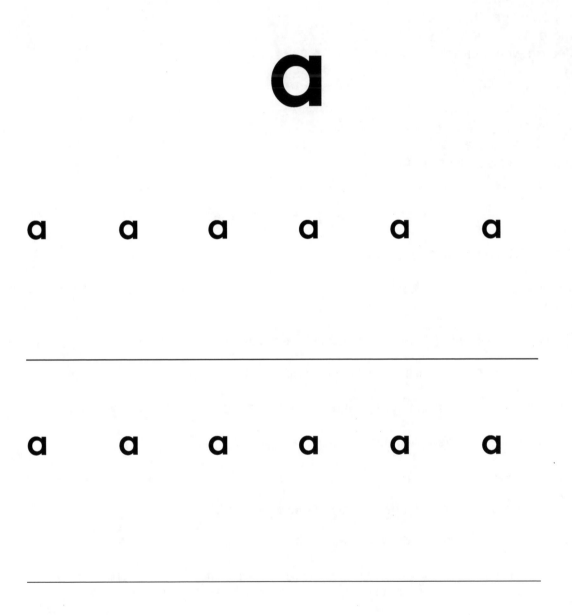

**Have the child practice writing this letter on a separate piece of wide-lined paper, saying the sound as he writes.**

# Word Fun

Have the child say the sounds these letters stand for.

**p**　　　**t**　　　**o**　　　**m**　　　**n**　　　**a**

Have the child read the sounds separately for each pair of words.  Then push the sounds together to make the word:  /**a**/---/**n**/　 '**an**'.

Tell the child that the first letter in a name is "tall" and sits on the line.  It is called a **capital letter**.

| | | | |
|---|---|---|---|
| a---n | an | o---n | on |
| a---m | am | a---t | at |
| n---o---t | not | t---a---p | tap |
| m---o---p | mop | p---a---n | pan |
| p---a---t | pat | m---a---n | man |
| m---a---t | mat | n---a---p | nap |
| m---a--p | map | t---a---n | tan |
| a---n---t | ant | | |
| P---a---m | Pam | T---o---m | Tom |

## Special word.　　　a
　　**Say**: This says 'uh'.

**Have the child copy each word onto a piece of lined paper.  Dictate some words for him to write from memory.  Make sure he says the sound out loud as he writes each letter.**

# Really Reading

Reading words with the sounds: **p t o m n a**

Pat at a nap on a mat

Tom at a map

a tot on a pot

a tan man on a mat

an ant on a pan

an ant on Pam

## the sound /d/    The Last Dinosaur in the World

Read the story for enjoyment.  Do the listening exercise.  Read the story again and ask the child to signal when he hears the sound /d/.  [Make it short.  Don't say 'dee' or 'duh'] Play a game by having the child signal each time he hears the sound /d/.   Read the whole story after the lesson is over.

**DINK-DINK   DONK-DONK**
**DINK-DINK   DONK-DONK**

The sound went on for days and days.
The ground moved.  The trees swayed.
The water danced on Dildee pond.
Dan dog hid in the barn at Mr. Dole's farm.

The ducks and the drakes got dizzy.
The geese were in a tizzy.
The doves didn't coo
And the cows didn't moo.

---

### Listening for the Sound /d/

**Read each sentence to your child.**

The sound you hear the most in this story is /**d**/.  [Don't say 'duh.']

Watch my mouth when I say this sound:  /**d**/.  Now you say the sound /**d**/.  [Make sure it sounds like you said it.]

Say the word '**dog**' and listen for the sound /**d**/.  Does it come first or last?

Say the word '**pond**' and listen for the sound /**d**/.  Does it come first or last?  Raise your hand when you hear the sound /**d**/.  Listen while I say it slowly:

     **p---o---n---d**          Listen when I push the sounds together:     **pond**

Say the word '**dandy**' and listen for the sound /**d**/.  The sound /**d**/ comes in two places in this word.  Listen while I say it slowly:

     **d---a---n---d---y**

Say the sounds slowly with me this time.     **d---a---n---d---y**

Now you push the sounds together and say the word.
-------------------------------------------------------------------------------------
If the child needs extra practice, do more words with /**d**/.  Reread the story and play the listening game.   Do the "Write It, Say It" exercise for the sound /**d**/.

## Write It, Say It

Have the child should trace the large letter with his finger, saying the sound out loud, then copy each letter on the line below.  Be sure the letter **d** sits on the line.

# d

d   d   d   d   d   d

_____

d   d   d   d   d   d

_____

Have the child practice writing this letter on a separate piece of wide-lined paper.

## the sound /i/    Six Wicked Witches

Read the story for enjoyment.  Do the listening exercise.  Read the story again and ask the child to listen for the sound /i/.  Don't say the letter name.  Play a game by having the child signal each time she hears the sound /i/.   [The word pretty sounds "pritty" ].  Read the whole story after the lesson is over.

Six wicked witches live in a den.
It's a pity, they're not pretty.
They're tall, and skinny, and thin.

Princess Imogen Pippin,
is little and pretty
with a dimple in her chin.

The six wicked witches hate Princess Imogen.
"We don't like her.  We don't like her one bit.
We'll get rid of this pretty Miss
Imogen Pippin, princess!"

---

## Listening for the Sound /i/

**Read each sentence to your child.**

The sound you hear the most in this story is /i/ [Don't say the letter name.  It's the wrong sound.]

Watch my mouth when I say this sound:  /i/.  Now you say the sound /i/

Say the word 'in' and listen for the sound /i/.  /i/ is the first sound.

Say the word 'witch' and listen for the sound /i/.  /i/ comes in the middle of the word.

When I say the word 'witch' put up your hand when you hear the sound /i/.
I'm going to say each sound slowly [tch is one sound]:

**w--i--tch**

Now you push the sounds together and say the word.

---

If the child needs extra practice, do more words with /i/.  When the child has mastered this, reread the story and play the listening game.  Do the "Write It, Say It" exercise for the sound /i/.

# Write It, Say It

Have the child should trace the large letter with his finger, saying the sound out loud, then copy each letter on the line below.   Always use lower case.  Make sure the letter **i** sits on the line.

_____


_____

**Have the child practice writing this letter on a separate piece of wide-lined paper.**

# Word Fun

Say the sounds these letters stand for.

**p      t      o      m      n      a      d      i**

Read the sounds separately for each pair of words.  Then push the sounds together to make the word:  **/i/---/n/**   'in'.

| | | | |
|---|---|---|---|
| **i---n** | **in** | **i---t** | **it** |
| **p---i---n** | **pin** | **d---i---d** | **did** |
| **d---a---d** | **dad** | **p---i---t** | **pit** |
| **t---i---p** | **tip** | **d---i---p** | **dip** |
| **d---o---t** | **dot** | **n---i---p** | **nip** |
| **m---a---d** | **mad** | **d---i---n** | **din** |
| **d---i---m** | **dim** | **p---a---d** | **pad** |
| **a---n---d** | **and** | **p---o---n---d** | **pond** |
| **T---o---d** | **Tod** | **T---i---m** | **Tim** |

**Special words:**       do           to
  Say, this is:       doo         too

Have the child copy each word onto a piece of lined paper.  Dictate some words to write from memory.  Make sure the child says the sound out loud as each letter is written.

# Really Reading

Reading words with the sounds:  p  t  o  m  n  a  d  i

an ant did nip dad

an ant did not nip Pam

it did not nip Tom

Tom and Pam dip a tin pan in a pond

Tom and Pam tip it on dad

Tom and Pam tip it on a tan man on a mat

## the sound /g/        Greg's Goat

Read the story for enjoyment.  Do the listening exercise.  Read the story again and ask the child to listen for the sound **/g/**. [Keep this sound short.  Don't say 'gee' or 'guh.']  . Read the whole story after the lesson is over.

Greg had a goat named Grace.
Grace used to graze on grass.
But by the time she was grown,
The grass was long gone.

The ground in the garden
Had begun to harden.
The garden was gray and not greening,
But Grace kept greedily eating.

Her body got longer.
Her teeth got bigger and stronger.
Grace gulped everything in sight.
Creatures great and small took flight.

---

### Listening to the Sound /g/

**Read each sentence to your child.**

The sound you hear the most in this story is **/g/**. [Say **/g/** as quickly as possible.  Don't say 'guh'.]

Watch my mouth when I say this sound: **/g/** [Open your mouth wide.]

Now you say the sound **/g/** [Make sure it sounds like you said it.]

Say the word '**goat**' and listen for the sound **/g/**.  Is **/g/** the first or the last sound in '**goat**'?

Say the word '**pig**' and listen for the sound **/g/**.  Is **/g/** the first or the last sound in '**pig**'?

Say the word '**bigger**' and listen for the sound **/g/**.  Now **/g/** is in the middle.  Listen while I say it slowly ['bigger' has four sounds]:

       **b---i---gg---er**

Now you push the sounds together and say this word.

---

If your child needs extra practice, do more words with **/g/**.  Reread the story and play the listening game.  Do the "Write It, Say It" exercise for the sound **/g/.**

## Write It, Say It

Have the child trace the large letter with a finger, saying the sound out loud.  Copy each letter on the line below.  Use lower case with the tail of the **g** falling below the line.

g    g    g    g    g    g

_____

g    g    g    g    g    g

_____

Have the child practice writing this letter on a separate piece of wide-lined paper.

## the sound /b/          Billy is Saved from a Bear

Read the story for enjoyment.  Do the listening exercise.  Read the story again and ask the child to listen for the sound /**b**/.  [Make it as short.  Don't say 'bee' or 'buh.'}.   Read the story again and play the listening game.  Read the whole story after the lesson is over.

Robbie and Brian and Billy
were the best boys they could be.
Dad said, "Because you boys are the best,
I'm taking you out West.
We're off to the Rocky Mountains
To the land of the Blackhawk Indians.

On top of the mountains, the sun beamed bright.
The boys saw a beautiful sight.
The boys saw a lake that was bluer than blue.
By a babbling brook, the buttercups bloom.
Nearby, a beaver was building a dam.
A bighorn sheep watched with her lamb.
Away from the lake, by the river bend
A badger dozed beside his den.
A bald eagle burst from the trees
And glided away on the evening breeze.

---

### Listening for the Sound /b/

**Read each sentence to the child.**

The sound you hear the most in this story is /**b**/.  [Don't say 'buh.']

Watch my mouth when I say this sound: /**b**/.  Now you say the sound /**b**/ [Make sure it sounds like you said it.]

Say the word '**boy**' and listen to the sound /**b**/.  Is it the first or the last sound?

Say the word '**sob**' and listen to the sound /**b**/.  Is it the first sound or the last sound?

Listen while I say the word '**babble.**' How many /**b**/ sounds do you hear?  Raise your hand when you hear the sound /**b**/.  I'm going to say the word slowly.  [There are five sounds.]

      **b---a---bb---u---l**

Now push the sounds together and say the word.

---

If the child needs extra practice, do more words with /**b**/.  Do the "Write It, Say It" exercise for the sound /**b**/.

# Write It, Say It

Have the child should trace the large letter with his finger, saying the sound out loud, then copy each letter on the line below.  Always use lower case with the letter **b** sitting on the line.

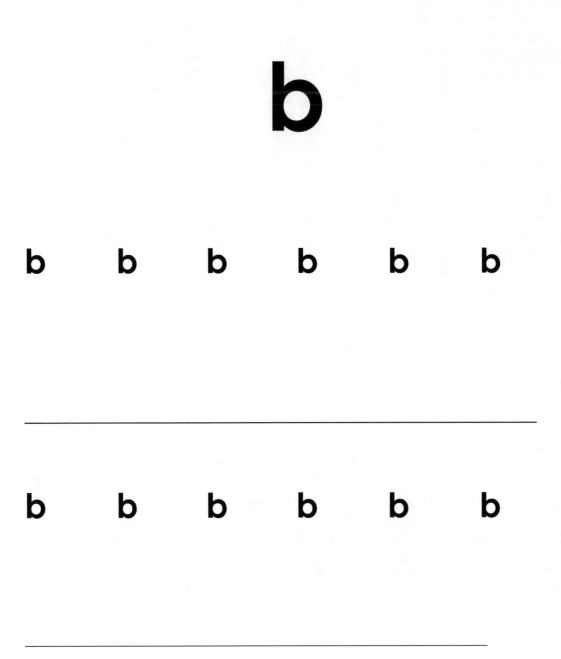

**Have the child practice writing this letter on a separate piece of wide-lined paper.**

# Word Fun

Say the sounds these letters stand for:

**p   t   o   m   n   a   d   l   g   b**

Have the child read the words slowly one sound at a time and then push the sounds together to make the word.

| | | | |
|---|---|---|---|
| b---a---d | bad | g---o---t | got |
| b---i---t | bit | b---i---g | big |
| p---i---g | pig | d---o---g | dog |
| b---a---t | bat | t---a---g | tag |
| b---i---b | bib | d---i---g | dig |
| m---o---b | mob | b---a---g | bag |

## Special word: **go**
   Say, this is: 'go'

Have the child copy each word onto a piece of lined paper, and then write some of the words from memory as you dictate. Make sure he says the sound out loud as each letter is traced or written.

# Really Reading
Reading words with the sounds: p t o m n a d i g b

dad got Tom a dog

mom got a dog tag

dog did dig and dig

dog did dig a big pit

dog got in it and a pig got in it

dog bit pig

bad dog


Tom got a bat

dog go t it

dog got a bat into a pond

bad dog


Tom got a big bag

dog bit it

dog got in it

bad dog

## the sound /u/    Uttley Meets a Bunch of Bunnies

Read the story for enjoyment.  Do the listening exercise.  Read the story again and ask the child to listen for the sound **/u/**--'uh.'  [Don't say the letter name.  It's the wrong sound.]  Watch out. The sound **/u/** can also be spelled: **o** (*once, one*), **ou** (*young, country*).   Play the listening game.  Read the whole story after the lesson is over.

Once upon a time there was a puppy.
His name was Uttley.
Uttley was chubby and young.
He was not quite one.

One lovely, sunny Sunday
Uttley thought he'd run to the country.
Uttley dug under the gate
Sometime around eight.

Uttley ran too far and too much.
He began to huff and puff.
He started to stumble.
His tummy began to rumble.

---

### Listening for the Sound /u/

### Read each sentence to your child.

The sound you hear the most in this story is /**u**/. [Don't say the letter name.]

Watch my mouth when I say this sound: /**u**/.  Now you say the sound /**u**/.

Say the word '**up**' and listen for the sound /**u**/.  Is /**u**/ the first sound or the last sound in the word '**up**?'

Say the word '**tub**' and listen for the sound /**u**/.  /**u**/ is the middle sound in '**tub**.'

Listen while I say the word slowly: **t---u---b**  Raise your hand when you hear the sound /**u**/.

Say the word '**puppy**' and listen for the sound /**u**/.  Listen while I say the word slowly. Raise your hand when you hear the sound /**u**/.

   **p---u---pp---y**

Now you push the sounds together to say the word.

-------------------------------------------------------------------------

If the child needs more practice, do more words with the sound /**u**/.  Do the 'Write, Say It' exercise.

## Write It, Say It

Have the child should trace the large letter with his finger, saying the sound out loud, then copy each letter on the line below.   Always use lower case.  Make sure the letter **u** sits on the line.

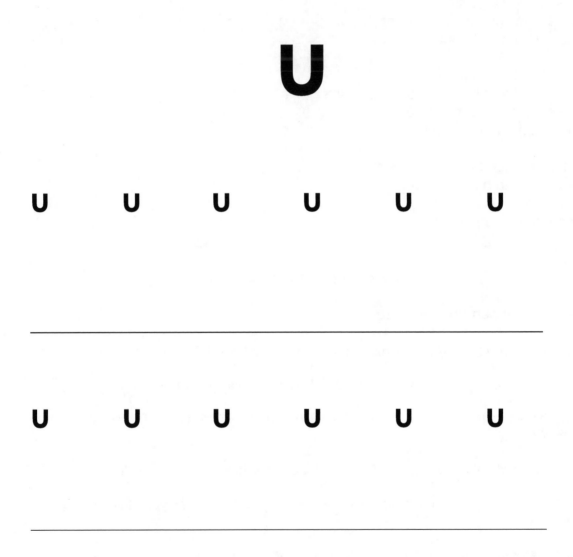

**Have the child practice writing this letter on a separate piece of wide-lined paper.**

# Word Fun

Say the sounds these letters stand for.

p    t    o    m    n    a    d    i    g    b    u

Have the child read the words one sound at a time and then push the sounds together to make the word.

| | | | |
|---|---|---|---|
| u---p | up | b---u---t | but |
| d---u---g | dug | p---u---p | pup |
| m---u---d | mud | t---u---b | tub |
| g---u---m | gum | n---u---t | nut |
| t---u---g | tug | b---u---g | bug |

**Special Word:  put**
Say: This says   'poot' (as in *soot*)

Have the child copy each word onto a piece of lined paper.  Have her write some of the words from memory as you dictate.  Make sure she says the sound out loud as each letter is written.

# Really Reading

Reading words with the sounds: **p t o m n a d i g b u**

Help with capital letters for **Mom** and **Dad.**    Special word for this story:  **'put'**

Dad got Pam a pup

Mom got pup a tag


pup and dog dig and dig

dog dug up a big bug

pup dug up a nut


dog dug and dug

dog dug a big pit

pup and dog got in it

dog got up


but pup got in mud

pup did not get up

pup did not get up on top


dad got pup up

dad put pup in a tub

dad put pup on a mat

mom and dad did pat and pat

pup had a big nap

## the sound /e/    Ellie Elephant Saves Edward Leopard

Read the story for enjoyment. Do the listening exercise. Read the story again and ask the child to listen for the sound /e/. [Don't say the letter name. It's the wrong sound.] Watch out. The sound /e/ can also be spelled **ea** (h*ea*ding, f*ea*thery). Have the child signal each time she hears the sound /e/. Read the whole story after the lesson is over.

One wet Wednesday
Edward Leopard sat in his den.
When the rain stopped
he went off to explore, about ten.

He sped off to the forest.
He was heading west.
The feathery grass smelled fresh
as it bent against his chest.

When he got to the forest,
Edward never knew
a trap was set,
hidden from view.

---

### Listening for the Sound /e/

**Read each sentence to your child.**

The sound you heard the most in this story is /**e**/. [Don't say the letter name.]

Watch my mouth when I say this sound: /**e**/. Now you say the sound /**e**/.

Say the word '**end**'. Is /**e**/ the first sound or the last sound?

Say the word '**elephant**' and listen to the first sound. The sound /**e**/ is the first sound in '**elephant**' too.

Say the word '**net**'. The sound /**e**/ is the middle sound in '**net**.'
Listen while I say it slowly:

    **n---e---t**          Now push the sounds together to make the word.

Listen to this word while I say the sounds slowly.

    **l---e---ss---o---n**     Let's push the sounds together to make this word.

---

If necessary do more words with the sound /e/. Do the story listening game. Then do the Write It, Say It exercise for the sound /e/.

# Write It, Say It

Have the child should trace the large letter with his finger, saying the sound out loud, then copy each letter on the line below.   Always use lower case.  Make sure the letter e sits on the line.

e

e    e    e    e    e    e

_____

e    e    e    e    e    e

_____

**Have the child practice writing this letter on a separate piece of wide-lined paper.**

# Word Fun

Say the sounds these letters stand for.

**p    t    o    m    n    a    d    i    g    b    u    e**

Have the child read the words slowly one sound at a time and then push the sounds together to make the word.

b---e---d        bed                    p---e---t        pet

g---e---t        get                    t---e---n        ten

m---e---t        met                    d---e---n        den

p---e---n        pen                    n---e---t        net

p---e---p        pep                    m---e---n        men

e---n---d        end                    T---e---d        Ted

b---e---n---d    bend                   t---e---n---t    tent


**Special words:**        **be**          **me**
Say, this word is:        bee             mee

Have the child copy each word onto a piece of lined paper, and then write some of the words from memory as you dictate. Make sure he says the sound for each letter as he writes it.

**Really Reading**
Reading words with the sounds: **p t o m n a d i g b u e**

## At The Big Top

Pam and Tom met Ted at a big tent

Pam and Tom and Ted got in


ten men got up on top in a big tent

ten men dip and bend

ten men end up in a net


big men tug and tug

big men tug on and on

big men tip into a pond


a pig got a mop

a dog got a mop

a pig and a dog mop up


Pam and Tom got to bed at ten

# Section II

## Teaching the Sounds

/h/  /w/  /r/  /j/  /v/  /z/  /l/  /f/  /s/

### Plus:

## Consonant Crunch and Plurals

## Parents/Teachers

This section completes the consonant sounds that are spelled with one letter or with double letters. The vowel sounds remain the same.

So far, children have learned the consonant sounds with mainly one spelling, along with the simple logic: **one sound/one spelling, anywhere in the word.**

In this section, there are some exceptions to this principle. Several consonants can come at the beginning and in the middle or words, but never at the end: like **/h/** and **/w/** . Some consonants, like **/v/** and **/j/**, are spelled differently at the beginnings and ends of words (**v**ery/ser**ve**, **j**ump/fu**dge**) For now, children will be learning only words with these sounds in *initial position*.

Several consonants are spelled with double letters. This happens in the middle or ends of words, but never at the beginning, as with the sounds **/z/ /f/ /l/** and **/s/**. Double letter spellings will be taught in these lessons.

None of this will affect the *listening exercises* for the child, but will affect Word Fun and Really Reading. Instructions are provided throughout the lessons to make these issues clear.

**Dialect.** Some dialects make a distinction between the sounds **/w/** (*wind*) and **/wh/** (*when*). Only the **/w/** sound is taught here. Children automatically adjust speech sounds to fit their dialect.

**Writing**. Writing exercises continue, but only a sample letter is shown. Continue this exercise exactly as before by using a separate piece of wide-lined paper. Write the sample letter at the top of the paper, making sure it 'sits' on the line correctly. Children should copy this example many times.

**Original writing.** Children who make good progress will want to write words and simple sentences using the words they have learned so far. Monitor the child's written work. Make sure that *possible* spellings are used instead of just guessing. It's OK if a spelling is wrong (for now) but not OK if the spelling is impossible (illegal).

**Storybook.** **Please remember to read the complete story after every lesson. This reminder will be dropped from the instructions at this point.**

## the sounds /h/ and /w/       Harper Was a Hero

**This story features two sounds.**   Teach only one sound at a time.  Do the second sound on a different day.  Follow the usual procedure:  Read the story for enjoyment. Do the listening exercise for the sound **/h/** on day 1.   Read the story again and play the listening game.  The child should listen for the sound **/h/** [a 'huff' of air].  Do Write It, Say It for **h**.

**On the next day or the day after,** read the same story and ask the child to listen to the sound **/w/**.  Do the listening exercise for **/w/** [lips form '*w*' and release with a puff of air]. Finish with the usual exercises.

Henry lived high on a hill
at Hillhead House,
with his mom and dad,
and Harper, his horse.

One warm day, Harper and Henry
rode off in perfect weather.
They went whistling down the hill
through the hayfields and heather.

Henry wanted to fly like the wind.
Harper hurdled over hedges,
over water holes and wire fences,
through the woods, ducking branches.

---

### Listening for the Sound /h/

**Read each sentence below to the child.**

Watch my mouth when I say this sound: **/h/** [open mouth, a huff of air]

Now you say the sound /**h/. This sound comes at the beginnings and the middle of words, but never at the end.**

Say the word '**house**' and listen for the sound /**h/.**  Say the name '**Harper**' and listen for the sound /**h/.**   Think of some other words that start with the sound /**h/.**

[Spend as much time on this as you need to.]

---

Reread the story and play the listening game for the sound /**h/.**  Do the Write it, Say It exercise for **h.**

## Write It, Say It

Transfer this letter to a piece of wide-lined paper, making sure it sits on the line. Have the child copy this many times, saying the sound as he writes.

---

## Listening for the Sound /w/

**Read the Harper story again and ask the child to listen to the sound /w/. Follow the same directions as above.**

**Read each sentence below to the child.**

Watch my mouth when I say this sound: /**w**/ [lips form 'oo' then a huff of air]

Now you say the sound /**w**/. This sound comes at the beginnings of words and not at the end.

Say the word '**wall**' and listen for the sound /**w**/. Say the word '**winter**' and listen for the sound /**w**/. Now think of some other words that start with the sound /**w**/.

[Spend as much time on this as you need to.]

-------------------------------------------------------------------------------------

Reread the story and play the listening game for the sound /**w**/. Then show your child the letter for the sound /**w**/ on the next page. Say: This letter is for the sound /**w**/." Do the Write It, Say It exercise for the sound /**w**/.

---

## Write It, Say It

Transfer this letter to a piece of wide-lined paper, making sure it sits on the line. Have the child copy this many times, saying the sound as he writes.

---

# Word Fun

Say the sounds these letters stand for:

p    t    o    m    n    a    d    i    g    b    u    u    e    h    w

Children should say each word slowly one sound at a time then push the sounds together to make the word.

| | | | |
|---|---|---|---|
| h---a---d | had | h---i---m | him |
| h---a---t | hat | h--o---p | hop |
| h--o---t | hot | h---o---g | hog |
| h---e---n | hen | h---i---t | hit |
| h---a---m | ham | h---i---d | hid |
| h---u---t | hut | h---u---g | hug |
| h---a---n---d | hand | h---u--n---t | hunt |

| **Special words:** | **he** | **the** |
|---|---|---|
| SAY: this word is | hee | thuh |

| | | | |
|---|---|---|---|
| w---e---b | web | w---i--n | win |
| w---e---t | wet | w---i--g | wig |
| w---i---n---d | wind | w--e---n---t | went |

| **Special words:** | **we** | **when** |
|---|---|---|
| SAY: this word is | wee | wen |

Child should copy these words onto lined paper. Do spelling dictation, mixing the **/h/** and **/w/** words. Children should sound out each letter as they write.

53

# Really Reading

Reading words with the sounds: p t o m n a d i g b u e h w

hen had on a hat

hen did hum

hen went hop hop hop in a hat


a big wind got up

a big wind hit hen

up up up went the hat

the hat went into the pond


hen went to get the hat

but hen did not get it

hog went in and he got wet

but hog got the hat


hog got a big hand

hog got a big hug

**the sound /r/**             **The Rescue**

Read the story.  Do the listening exercise.  Read the story again, and ask the child to listen for the *sound* **/r/**.   Have the child signal each time he hears the sound **/r/**.

It rained and rained.  The river was rising.
The river rushed and roared.
Water rippled over the shore.

Lightening struck like a rocket.
The thunder rolled.  It rattled and rumbled.
It growled and grumbled.

Reginald Reindeer went to peer at the river.
He heard the river roar.
He saw the water rising over the shore.

---

### Listening to the Sound /r/

**Read each sentence below to the child.**

The sound you hear the most in this story is **/r/**.  [Don't say 'er'.  Say 'wr' with lips rounded.  Keep it short.]

Watch my mouth when I say this sound: **/r/**  Now you say the sound **/r/**.  [Make sure it sounds like you said it.]

Say the word **'ram'** and listen for the sound **/r/**.   Now say the word **'rain'** and listen for the sound **/r/.**

Think of some other words that start with the sound **/r/.**  Spend as much time as you need on this.

---

Reread the story and do the listening exercise.  Do the Write It, Say It exercise for the sound **/r/**.

## Write It, Say It

Transfer this letter to a piece of wide-lined paper.  Make sure it sits on the line. Have the child copy this many times, saying the sound as he writes.

r

# Word Fun

Say the sounds that these letters stand for:

p   t   o   m   n   a   d   i   g   b   u   e   h   w   r

Have the child read the words slowly one sound at a time, and push the sounds together to make the word.

| | | | |
|---|---|---|---|
| r---u---n | run | r---a---n | ran |
| r---a---p | rap | r---o---t | rot |
| r---a---m | ram | r---a---g | rag |
| r---o---b | rob | r---a---t | rat |
| r---i---b | rib | r---i---p | rip |
| r---u---g | rug | r---e---d | red |
| g---r---a---b | grab | t---r---i---p | trip |

**Special Word:**   **her**
SAY, this word is    'her'

Have the child copy each word on a piece of lined paper.  Do spelling dictation.  She should say each sound out loud as each letter is traced or written.

# Really Reading

Reading words with the sounds: **p t o m n a d i g u e h w r**

[Help read the capital **R** in 'Ron.'  Explain that all names start with a 'big' letter.]

**Ron rat was in a band**

**Ron had a big red drum**

**when he hit the drum**

**it went bim bam bop**

**it went rim rap rop**


**Ron rat and the band went on a trip**

**he and the band had a big hit**

**Ron had fun**

## the sound /j/          Just July

Read the story for enjoyment.  Do the listening exercise.  Read the story again and ask your child to listen to the sound **/j/**.  [ **Watch out**: **/j/** is spelled 4 ways in this story:  **j**, (*j*ust), **g** (*g*iant), **ge** (cotta*ge*) and **dge** (bri*dge*).]

Janet and Jill lived in Jewel Cottage
in the shade of a giant oak,
up on the ridge by Juniper Bridge,
at the edge of Jasper Gorge.

One gorgeous day in July
with a gentle breeze and sapphire sky,
Janet and Jill were on top of the jungle gym
when their Mom called them in.

"Jump down," she said.
"I've got a job for two little girls.
Come and join in
I need some help in the kitchen."

---

### Listening for the sound /j/

**Read each sentence to your child.**

The sound you heard the most is **/j/** [Keep it short.  Try not to say 'juh.']

Watch my mouth when I say this sound: **/j/.**  Now you say the sound **/j/.**  [Make sure it sounds like you said it.]

Say the word '**jam**' and listen for the sound **/j//.**  Does it come first or last?

Say the word '**jump**' and listen for the sound **/j/.**  Does it come first or last?

Say the word '**fudge**' and listen for the sound **/j/.**  Does it come first or last?

The sound **/j/** can come anywhere in a word, but it's spelled differently at the ends of words.  Right now we will learn only the words that start with the sound **/j/.**  Can you think of some other words that start with the sound **/j/**?

[Spend as much time as you need to.]

-------------------------------------------------------------------------------------
Reread the story and do the listening exercise.  Do the Write It, Say It exercise for the sound **/j/.**

## Write It, Say It

Transfer this letter to a page of wide-lined paper, making sure it hangs below the line. Have the child copy this many times, saying the sound as he writes.

# j

---

## Word Fun

Say the sounds that these letters stand for:

p t o m n a d i g b u e h w r j

Have the child read the words slowly one sound at a time, then push the sounds together to make the word.

| | | | |
|---|---|---|---|
| j---i---g | jig | j---a---m | jam |
| j---o---t | jot | j---o---b | job |
| j---o---g | jog | j---a---b | jab |
| j---u---g | jug | j---e---t | jet |
| j---u---m---p | jump | | |
| J---a---n | Jan | J---i---m | Jim |

Have the child copy each word onto a piece of lined paper. Dictate some spelling words from the list. Children should say each sound out loud as they write it.

# Really Reading

Reading words with the sounds: p t o m n a d i g b u e h w r j

Jan had red jam in a big jug

the pup ran up

pup did jig and jog

pup did jump up on Jan

Jan did drop the jam

Jan got jam on the rug

pup got jam on him

pup got jam on Jan


Jan had to mop it up

but Jan did a bad job

and mom got mad

## the sounds /v/ and /z/   The Driving Lesson

**This story features two sounds**. Read the story for enjoyment. Do the listening exercise for the sound **/v/**. Repeat this story on another day for the sound **/z/**.

Victor Beaver lived high above a valley.
In a cozy house under the river Torrey.
Victor Beaver drove a little van.
He helped other beavers fix their dams.

One day, down in the valley,
a carnival came to the village green.
Zeke Weasel said to his sister Zoe,
"Let's borrow Victor Beaver's van.
We can drive to the carnival."

---

### Listening for the Sound /v/

**Read each sentence to your child.**

One sound you heard a lot in this story was **/v/.** [Say '**vvv**'. Don't say 'vuh']

Watch my mouth when I say this sound: /**v**/ [upper teeth on lower lip]

Now you say the sound /**v**/. Say the word '**van**' and listen for the sound /**v**/. Is /**v**/ the first sound or the last sound?

Now say the word '**live**' ['liv']. Is the sound /**v**/ the first sound or the last sound?

I am going to say the next word slowly. Raise your hand when you hear the sound /**v**/.
**s---e---v---e---n**

Now you push the sounds together and say this word.

The sound /**v**/ can come anywhere in a word. It has a different spelling at the ends of words. For now, we'll learn only the words that start with the sound /**v**/.

Think of some other words that start with the sound /**v**/.

---

Reread the story and play the listening game. Do the Write It, Say It exercise for the sound /**v**/.

## Write It, Say It

Transfer this letter to a page of wide-lined paper, making sure it sits on the line. Have the child copy this many times, saying the sound as he writes.

# V

---

## Listening for the Sound /z/

Read the story again, and ask the child to listen for the sound **/z/**. [**Watch out**. The sound **/z/** is spelled two ways in this story: **z**, **s**.] Do the listening exercise.

**Read each sentence below to the child.**

This time you were listening for the sound **/z/** [Say 'zzz' and not 'zuh.']

Watch my mouth when I say this sound: **/z/** [teeth clenched and smile]

Now you say the sound **/z/**. Is the sound **/z/** the first or the last sound in **zip**?

Is the sound **/z/** the first or the last sound in **froze?**

I'm going to say the next word slowly. Raise your hand when you hear the sound **/z/**.
f—u—zz—y

Now push the sounds together and say this word.

---

If the child needs extra practice, do more words with **/z/.** Reread the story and play the listening game.

## Write It, Say It

Transfer this letter to a piece of wide-lined paper, making sure it sits on the line. Have the child copy this many times, saying the sound as he writes.

# Z

# Word Fun

**The Sounds /v/ and /z/**

p  t  o  m  n  a  d  i  g  b  u  e  h  w  r  v  z

Have the child read the words one sound at a time and then push the sounds together to make the word.  **NEW**:  the sound **/z/** is spelled with double letters at the end of these words.  This is still one sound.

| | | | |
|---|---|---|---|
| v---a---n | van | v---e---t | vet |
| v---a---t | vat | | |

| | | | |
|---|---|---|---|
| z---i---g | zig | z---a---g | zag |
| z---i---p | zip | | |

| | | | |
|---|---|---|---|
| b---u---zz | buzz | f---u---zz | fuzz |
| f---i---zz | fizz | | |

Do the copying and spelling activities.  The child should say the sound out loud as each letter is written.  Double letters = one sound.

# Really Reading

Reading words with the sounds: **p t o m n a d i g b u e h w r j v z**

a big bug had fuzz

a big bug went buzz

zap—

the big bug bit Tom

Tom went zig-zag

Tom did not get up


a man had a red van

he went to get the vet

the vet had a tan bag

zip--

the vet dug in the bag


Tom got a jab

Tom got up

Tom did jump and run

## the sound /l/    Lionel's Yellow Balloon

Read the story for enjoyment.  Do the listening exercise.  Read the story again and listen for the sound /l/.  Have the child signal each time he hears the sound /l/.

Lionel Elephant lived in Amboseli
with his wife Nell and little Ellie.
One day he looked up at a flock of flamingos.
"Look at those lucky birds, flying to and fro."

Lionel longed to fly.
He said, "If birds can fly, so can I.
Elephants learn fast.  Elephants are clever.
Elephants never say 'never.'"

---

**Listening for the Sound /l/**

**Read each sentence to your child.**

The sound you hear the most in this story is the sound /l/  [Flip your tongue down.  Don't say 'el' or 'ul' .  Keep it short.  Try not to say 'luh'.]

Watch my mouth when I say this sound: /l/.  Now you say the sound /l/.

Say the word **'luck'** and listen for the sound /l/.  Is it the first sound or the last sound?

Say the word **'well'** and listen for the sound /l/.  Is it the first sound or the last sound?

Listen carefully while I say the next word slowly.  Raise your hand when you hear the sound /l/.

> **b—a—ll—oo—n**

Now let's push the sounds together to make the word.

---

Reread the story and do the listening game.  Do the Write It Say It exercise for the sound /l/.

## Write It, Say It

Transfer this letter to a piece of wide-lined paper, making sure it is tall and stands on the line.  Have the child copy this many times, saying the sound as he writes.

**l**

# Word Fun

Say these the sounds these letters stand for:

p  t  o  m  n  a  d  i  g  b  u  e  h  w  r  j  v  z  l

Children should say each word one sound at a time, then push the sounds together to make the word. **NOTE**: This sound can be spelled with double letters. Tell the child this is one sound.

| l---e---t | let | l---e---d | led |
| l---a---d | lad | l---i---d | lid |
| l---i---p | lip | l---o---t | lot |
| l---a---p | lap | l---e---g | leg |
| l---o---g | log | l---i---t | led |
| l---u---g | lug | p---l---o---p | plop |
| h---e---l---p | help | g---l---a---d | glad |
| w---e—ll | well | b---e---ll | bell |
| t---e---ll | tell | d---o---ll | doll |
| h---i---ll | hill | m---i---ll | mill |
| p---i---ll | pill | w---i---ll | will |
| g---u---ll | gull | N---e---ll | Nell |
| J---i---ll | Jill | B---i---ll | Bill |

Do the copying and spelling activities. Child should say the sound as each letter is written. Double letters = one sound.

# Really Reading

Reading words with the sounds: **p t o m n a d i g b  u e h w r j v z l**

dog and pup run a lot

dog and pup zig and zag

dog and pup jump and jog

dog and pup run up a hill


pup got up on a log

but pup fell and went plop

pup got a bad leg

pup had a limp


help   help


dog got Jill the vet

Jill did help pup get up

Jill had a big pill

the pill will help pup get well


pup had a nap

he will get well

dog will be glad

## the sound /f/    The Fable of the Fox and the Wolf

Read the story for enjoyment.  Do the listening exercise.  Read the story again and play the listening game.  Watch out.  Two ways to spell **/f/** here:  **f** and **gh** (rou*gh*, enou*gh*)

1. Wolf said to his friends,
"I'm far smarter than Fox.
In fact, Fox is a fool."
Fox said, "That's false,
and completely untrue."

2. "Foxes are famous for thinking of course.
A wolf gets his way by force.
But 'smart' doesn't mean fierce and rough.
That's not nearly good enough."

3. So deep in the forest
they set up a contest
to find out who was the smartest.

---

### Listening for the Sound /f/     Read each sentence below to the child.

The sound you hear the most in this story is **/f/**.  This sound can come anywhere in a word.  [To say **/f/** put your top teeth on your lower lip and blow air:  'ffffff'.  Don't say 'fuh']

Watch my mouth when I say this sound: **/f/.**  Now you say the sound **/f/.**

Say the word **'fox'** and listen for the sound **/f/.**  Is it the first sound or the last sound?

Say the word **'frog'** and listen for the sound **/f/.**  Is it the first or the last sound?

Say the word **'wolf'** and listen for the sound **/f/.**  Is it the first or the last sound?

Now I'm going to say a word slowly.  Raise your hand when you hear the sound **/f/.**
        **aw---f---u---l**

Now you push the sounds together and say the word.

---

If the child needs extra practice, do more words with **/f/.**  Reread the story and do the listening game.  Do the Write It, Say It exercise.

### Write It, Say It
Transfer this letter to a page of wide-lined paper, making sure it stands on the line.  Have the child copy this many times, saying the sound as he writes.

# Word Fun

Say the sounds these letters stand for:

p t o m n a d i g b u e h w r j v z l f

Children should read each word slowly, one sound at a time, then push the sounds together to make the word. **NOTE:** This sound is can be spelled with double letters in the middle or end of a word. Tell the child this is only one sound.

| | | | |
|---|---|---|---|
| i---f | if | f---i---t | fit |
| f---i---b | fib | f---e---d | fed |
| f---u---n | fun | f---a---n | fan |
| f---a---t | fat | f---i---g | fig |
| f---o---g | fog | f---r---o---g | frog |
| o---ff | off | f---i---ll | fill |
| f---e---ll | fell | m---u---ff | muff |
| h---u---ff | huff | p---u---ff | puff |
| f---i---zz | fizz | J---e---ff | Jeff |

**Special words:** of wolf from

Say, these words are: uv woolf frum

Do the copying and spelling activities, saying the sound out loud as each letter is being traced or written. Double letters stand for one sound.

# Really Reading

Reading words with the sounds: **p t o m n a d i g b u e h w r j v z l f**

Fred frog went in a pond

he got up on a log

he had fun

he did hop and jump on a log


a big bad wolf ran up


well well a fat frog on a log in a pond

it will be fun to get the frog off the log


wolf got in the pond and went to get the frog

he went huff and he went puff

but Fred did not fall off


wolf did lift the end of the log

and Fred fell off in the pond


but Fred frog got on a pad

Fred did jump from pad to pad

Fred hid in a bog

the big bad wolf did not get Fred

[Teacher: define the word 'bog.']

## the sound /s/    Sam's Famous Escape

Read the story for enjoyment.  Do the listening exercise.  Read the story again and ask the child to signal each time she hears the sound **/s/**.  [Watch out.  **/sh/** is not **/s/**.  **/s/** can be spelled **c** or **sc**.  Final **s** (the letter) can sound **/z/** at the ends of words: *'was'  'always'  'songs'  'lions'  'stairs'*]

1. Sam was a sea lion
the star of the show
when he was at Sea Land
long, long, ago

2. Sam took center stage
on time for each scene.
Sometimes he was funny.
Sometimes he was mean.

3. He barked at the walrus
always on cue
He swam and he splashed
like sea lions do.

4. He sang several songs.
He climbed up some stairs.
He blew a kiss to the crowd.
He tossed six balls in the air.

---

### Listening to the Sound /s/

**Read each sentence below to the child.**

The sound you hear the most in this story is **/s/**.  [Just hiss: **'sssss.'**  Don't say 'suh'.]

Watch my mouth when I say this sound: **/s/**  [teeth clenched and smile]

Now you say the sound **/s/**.  Say the word **'sea'** and listen for the sound **/s/**.

Say the word **'pass'** and listen for the sound **/s/**.  Is it the first sound or the last sound?

I'm going to say a word slowly.  Raise your had when you hear the sound **/s/**.
      l—o—s---t

Now push the sounds together and say the word.

---

If necessary, do more words with **/s/**.  Reread the story and do the listening game.   Do the Write It, Say It exercise.

## Write It, Say It
Transfer this letter to a piece of wide-lined paper, making sure it sits on the line.  Have the child copy this many times, saying the sound as he writes.

# Word Fun

Say the sounds these letters stand for:

**p   t   o   m   n   a   d   i   g   b   u   e   h   w   r   j   v   z   l   f   s**

Have the child read the words slowly one sound at a time and then push the sounds together to make the word. **NOTE:** This sound is can be spelled with double letters. **[UK dialect:** omit the words 'grass' and 'fast' or provide the correct pronunciation: 'grawss', 'fawst']

| | | | |
|---|---|---|---|
| u---s | us | s---a---t | sat |
| s---i---t | sit | s---a---g | sag |
| s---a---d | sad | b---u---s | bus |
| s---u---n | sun | s---o---b | sob |
| s---i---p | sip | s---e---ll | sell |
| t---o---ss | toss | m---i---ss | miss |
| l---e---ss | less | l---o---ss | loss |
| m---e---ss | mess | f---u---ss | fuss |
| d---r---e---ss | dress | s---t---i---ll | still |
| l---o---s---t | lost | s---o---f---t | soft |
| s---t---o---p | stop | s---l---i---p | slip |
| g---r---a---ss | grass | f---a---s---t | fast |
| g---u---s---t | gust | s---w---i---m | swim |

**Special words:**   as   has   his   is   was   saw
   Say, this sounds:   az   haz   hiz   iz   wuz   saw

[Explain:  Sometimes the sound **/z/** is spelled **s.**]

Do the copying and spelling activity.  Say the sound out loud as each letter is written. Double letters stand for one sound.

# Really Reading

Reading words with the sounds: **p t o m n a d i g b u e h w r j v z l f s**
*[Help with the words '**to**' and '**began**' in the story.]*

hen sat at a bus stop

hen had on a red dress and a sun hat

the bus did stop and hen got on

hen sat still on the bus


wolf saw hen get on the bus and he got on

wolf had on a dress and a wig

wolf did grab hen and jump off the bus

hen did fuss and fuss

hen went flap flap flap

wolf had to drop hen fast

but hen lost her hat

hen sat on the grass and began to sob


dog and pig saw the wolf run off

and hen sob and sit on the grass

dog and pig ran to get the wolf

and help hen get her hat

when wolf saw dog and pig

he began to run fast

but he lost his wig

and he fell on the grass

dog and pig sat on him

dog saw it was the big bad wolf


a gust of wind got the hat

a gust of wind did toss the hat into a pond

frog sat on a pad in the pond

frog will swim and get the hat

frog will help hen


hen got her hat and hen was glad

dog and pig got a big hug from hen

# Capital Letters and Punctuation


# Consonant Crunch


# Plurals

# Parents/Teachers

These Word Fun and Really Reading exercises provide practice at the next level of complexity: segmenting and blending longer words. **Do not skip these exercises.** Children must be secure in reading all the sounds represented by single and double letters. They must see how these sounds combine in longer words before moving on to the next level where one sound is represented by two different letters (*digraphs*). This initial practice is critical to allow the child to distinguish between adjacent consonants (two sounds) and consonant digraphs (one sound).

## Capital Letters and Punctuation

From now on, the Really Reading stories will include capital letters at the beginning of each sentence and proper punctuation. Many capital letters don't resemble lower case (**A  B  D  E  G  H  L  N  Q  R**), and children will need practice writing these new shapes. The first exercises in this section are for tracing or copying capital letters. If copying is easy for the child, have her copy each letter several times. If this is difficult, attach tracing paper and have her trace them. Explain what capital letters are for. Tell children: *"From now on the Really Reading stories use proper writing. In proper writing, each new idea starts with a big letter. We call these capital letters. When an idea ends, we put a dot. This dot is called a period. We're going to learn how to write the capital letters."*

Remind the child of these new concepts at each Really Reading exercise.

## Consonant Crunch

So far, children have learned 20 words with adjacent consonants. The goal of these lessons is to insure each child can read these words easily without your help. They do not need to know the word "consonant" right now. Tell the children that they will be learning longer words that have four or five sounds.

### Instructions
**Reading**. As before, words in the Word Fun exercises are set up in two groups. The first group is segmented. The second group are "practice words" written in the normal way.

*Segmented Words*: Read each sound separately. Push the sounds together to make the word (next column). Read the word again and slide a finger quickly under each letter as the word is read (demonstrate this). Read the word again, letting the eyes rather than the finger scan the letters. Now read the word at the normal rate. Repeat if necessary.

*Un-segmented Words:*
The child should read the word normally (fluently) at first try.  If this fails, segment the word sound-by-sound.  Blend the sounds back into the word.  Re-read the word until it is spoken at the normal rate.

**Writing**.  At the end of each reading exercise, have children copy as many words as they can onto a piece of lined paper.  **They must say each sound out loud as they write it.**  Dictate some of these words to spell from memory.

Consonant clusters are the hardest sounds to unglue, so give children lots of help.  If five-sound words are too hard right now, leave them for later.

## More Than One

There are several lessons on plurals.  Tell children that they can make words mean 'more than one' by adding the letter **s** at the end of a word.  [Plurals spelled **es** will be taught later].  The letter **s** can stand for either the sound  /**s**/ or /**z**/.

# CAPITAL LETTERS

The capital letters on this page are larger versions of the lower case letters the children already know.  Have children **copy each line on wide lined paper**, saying the sound as they write.  Cover lines below where they are working with a piece of blank paper.  Children should notice that capital letters are tall and stand on the line.

f  F          F    F    F    F    F    F    F    F    F

i  I          I    I    I    I    I    I    I    I

j  J          J    J    J    J    J    J    J    J

m  M          M    M    M    M    M    M    M    M

o  O          O    O    O    O    O    O    O    O

p  P          P    P    P    P    P    P    P    P

s  S          S    S    S    S    S    S    S    S

t  T          T    T    T    T    T    T    T    T

u  U          U    U    U    U    U    U    U    U

v  V          V    V    V    V    V    V    V    V

w  W          W    W    W    W    W    W    W    W

y  Y          Y    Y    Y    Y    Y    Y    Y    Y

z  Z          Z    Z    Z    Z    Z    Z    Z    Z

# CAPITAL LETTERS

These capital letters have **different shapes** to the lower case letters.  Teach this the same way as before.  Missing letters **c, k, q, x**  are taught later.

a A A A A A A A A A

b B B B B B B B B B

d D D D D D D D D D

e E E E E E E E E E

g G G G G G G G G G

h H H H H H H H H H

l L L L L L L L L L

n N N N N N N N N N

r R R R R R R R R R

# Word Fun

**REVIEW**.  Remind children they have seen these words before.  They should read this in the normal way, only 'sounding out' if necessary.

| | |
|---|---|
| ant | and |
| pond | end |
| bent | tent |
| stop | slip |
| wind | went |
| hunt | drum |
| fast | gust |
| glad | jump |
| frog | wolf |
| lost | plop |
| soft | still |
| grass | swim |
| dress | help |
| trip | from |

# Word Fun

## Four-sound words
## CCVC

Words on this page begin with two consonants in a row.  Follow the instructions in the Introduction to this section.  Have children read the word in a segmented way, and then blend  the sounds together.  If they have trouble blending two consonants provide lots of help.  *If necessary*, blend the word in two parts:

/f/  /l/ = 'fl'  --- /a/ /g/ = 'ag' ---------- 'fl'-'ag' =  'flag'.


f---l---a---g          flag                    s---t---a---g          stag

t---r---a--p           trap                    g---r---a---n          gran

t---r---a---m          tram                    d---r---i---p          drip

g---r---i--n           grin                    t---w---i---n          twin

s---p---i--n           spin                    s---p---i---ll         spill

s---l---e---d          sled                    p---l---u---m          plum


**Now copy words, saying each sound out loud.  Write from memory.**

# Word Fun
## More Four-sound Word Practice
## CCVC

Follow the instructions in the Introduction to this Section. If children have trouble reading these words, try blending the sounds in three steps as shown above.

| | |
|---|---|
| flat | drag |
| glad | flap |
| grab | snap |
| slam | swam |
| drop | spot |
| flop | slid |
| slug | sniff |
| stiff | fled |
| spell | step |
| floss | press |
| smell | sped |
| stuff | swell |
| plug | glum |

**Copy words, saying each sound.   Write from memory.**

# Word Fun
## Four-sound words
## CVCC

l---a---n---d     band         l---a---m---p     lamp

s---a---n---d     sand         h---a---n---d     hand

g---o---l---f     golf         m---a---s---t     mast

f---i---s---t     fist         g---i---f---t     gift

b---e---l---t     belt         n---e---s---t     nest

---

### More Four-sound Word Practice

| | |
|---|---|
| held | test |
| dent | must |
| sent | west |
| best | mend |
| bump | tilt |
| fond | limp |
| felt | last |
| self | rest |

Copy words, saying each sound out loud.  Write from memory

## Really Reading
### Four-sound Words

If a child struggles with a word, have her sound it out (segment), then blend it into the word. **No guessing.**   If this is hard, do each 'story' at a different time.

### Gran had a Swim

Gran went in and had a swim.
Gran swam fast.
Gran felt glad and had a grin.
Gran sat on soft flat sand.
Gran had a long rest.

### Tod had a Spill on a Tram

Tom Tod and Pam step up and jump on a tram.
The tram had a flag on top.
The flag will flap in the wind.
The tram went fast and Tom and Pam held on.
But Tod will not.
Tod was bad.
Tod did spin and jump.
Tod fell and got a bump.
Tod had a limp and his leg was stiff.

### Bill's Big Drum

Bill got a big drum as a gift.
Bill will be in a band.
But Bill did trip and drop the big drum.
The drum got bent.
A man had to lift it up.
The drum had a dent.
The man will help Bill mend it.

# Word Fun
## Optional: Five-sound Words
### CCVCC

**Blending five sound words is difficult. Stop if the child continues to have trouble.**

| | |
|---|---|
| b---l---o---n---d | blond |
| f---r---o---s---t | frost |
| t---r---a---m---p | tramp |
| s---t---a---m---p | stamp |
| s---t---u---m---p | stump |
| p---l---u---m---p | plump |

## Five-Sound Word Practice

| | |
|---|---|
| stomp | stand |
| grand | twist |
| drift | print |
| spilt | swept |
| swift | slept |
| spend | crust |

# Really Reading

## Optional: Mixing Four and Five-sound Words

Pat did not stand up in a gust of wind.
Pat fell in a big drift.

A plump, blond tot had a rest.
A plump, blond tot slept and slept.

Ned spilt it.
Ned swept it up.

A tramp sat on a big stump.
It was wet and the tramp got damp.
The tramp got stiff from the damp stump.

A van went west on a trip.
It sped on and on.
It was swift.
It slid in a frost.
Ten men will help the man in a van.

A stag was at a pond.
A stag did stand still.
It was grand.
Jill got a snap.
Jill will get a print.

# More Than One
## The Sound /s/

SAY: "We're going to read words that mean more than one thing.  We write "more than one" by adding the **letter <u>s</u>** at the end of the word."  (*Use letter name.*)

| | | | |
|---|---|---|---|
| tot | tots | pot | pots |
| mop | mops | ant | ants |
| mat | mats | bat | bats |
| pup | pups | nut | nuts |
| pet | pets | hat | hats |
| hut | huts | vet | vets |
| rat | rats | jet | jets |
| tent | tents | trap | traps |
| step | steps | spot | spots |

**Copy words, saying each sound out loud.  Write from memory.**

## More Than One
### The Sound /z/

SAY: "The **letter s** at the end of a word always means 'more than one.'   But in these words, the letter **s** sounds **/zzz/**."

| | | | |
|---|---|---|---|
| dog | dogs | fin | fins |
| pig | pigs | bib | bibs |
| bag | bags | tub | tubs |
| log | logs | bug | bugs |
| bed | beds | pen | pens |
| egg | eggs | hen | hens |
| hog | hogs | ram | rams |
| web | webs | van | vans |
| bell | bells | gull | gulls |
| doll | dolls | hill | hills |
| sled | sleds | plum | plums |
| drum | drums | frog | frogs |
| flag | flags | stag | stags |

# Really Reading
## More Than One

Start this lesson by teaching two new words.  They have 'funny' spellings and children will have to memorize them.   All words for plural ('more than one') in this story end in the *sound* **/s/**.   Help with apostrophe:  **Pat's hat**.

| | | |
|---|---|---|
| **Special words:** | **one** | **two** |
| Say, this word is: | wun | too |


One pup went up the steps and got on a tram.

One pup sat still.

Ten pups went up the steps and got on a tram.

Ten pups did not sit still.


Mom and Dad set up two tents.

One was for Tom and Pat.

Lots and lots of ants got in the tents.

Tom and Pat stamp on the ants.

Two rats got in.

The rats spill two pots.

Two rats sat on Pat's hat.

Dad set traps for the two rats.


Tom got ill.

Tom had lots of spots.

Tom must sit in bed.

# Really Reading

## More Than One

On this page, most plurals (but not all!) end in the *sound* /**z**/. Don't use the letter name. If necessary, say: "this sounds /**z**/ here."

Two hens sit in a pen.

Tom will get ten eggs from a nest.

Two eggs slip from his hand.

The two eggs drop. Plop.


Ten bugs sat on one log.

Six frogs jump on the log.

Two dogs flop on the log.

One pig stands on the end of the log.

The log tilts up.

The bugs and frogs and dogs and a pig all fall off.


Mom has two big bags.

Bess got one of Mom's bags.

It had two dolls in it.

One doll has two bells.

One doll has a red dress.

# Optional: The Vowel Sound /ah/ spelled <u>a</u>

In UK/Northeast US dialects, the letter **a** stands for the sound **/ah/** in some words. If this is true for you, tell the child the letter **a** in these words stands for **/ah/** (**not the /a/ in 'cat'**). *If this doesn't apply, children should read these words in the usual way.*

r---a---f---t          raft

g---r---a---ss        grass

m---a---s---t         mast

g---l---a---ss         glass

| | |
|---|---|
| pass | last |
| vast | fast |
| can't | brass |
| staff | blast |
| slant | can't |

Copy words, saying each sound out loud. Write from memory.

# Section III

## Introducing Sounds Spelled with Digraphs:

**(A 'digraph' is one sound spelled with two letters.)**

/k/   /sh/   /oo/   /<u>oo</u>/   /th/   /ng/   /ch/

# Parents/Teachers

**At this point children know how to read and write 21 of the 42 sounds in English, and can read and write 320 words. They know about plurals. They are familiar with lower and upper case letters, and how to mark the beginning and ending of sentences. Give them praise for a job well done.**

Take stock of the child's progress. A child should be able to read with moderate fluency all the Really Reading exercises so far. Spelling should be reasonably accurate. If children need more work, or a quick review, go back to the 'comfort zone' and work forward from there, reviewing Word Fun and Really Reading only. Handwriting may lag behind reading, more so for boys. Don't worry too much about this. Lots of handwriting practice is still to come.

The basic logic up to this point has been: **one-sound/one-letter, or one-sound/double letters.** This logic must be secure before a new logic is introduced. The remaining 21 sounds are spelled with letter-pairs known as **"digraphs."** The letter-pair stands for a sound that is *not* represented by either letter on its own, as in the spelling **sh** for the sound **/sh/** in '**ship**.'.

Your language is critical at this important step. The child has to remember which letters work together to stand for one sound and which do not. Pay close attention to the directions for the exercises. ***Understanding that two or more letters stand for one sound is a major key to unlocking our writing system.***

## Instructions

**Story fragment.** Read this in the usual way, first for enjoyment, and then as a listening exercise. Children can signal for each sound if they want to. Tell children they will hear the whole story later.

**Listening Exercise.** Carry out the scripted listening exercise for each sound as before. If your child needs more work, then add more words.

**Write It, Say It.** Children can write most letters by now. This means that the Write It, Say It activities are almost over. They appear here only for the lessons on the sound **/k/** and for the letter **y**.

**Word Fun Decoding**. Words are set out in two groups as before, segmented first, then blended together. There is also a set of non-segmented words. Children should read them in the normal way. If this is difficult, ask the child to segment the word, blend the sounds into the word, and say the word at the normal rate.

**Word Fun Copying and Spelling**. ***Never omit the copying and writing exercises***. Remember - writing doubles the speed to learn the written code.

Children should say each sound out loud as they write.  When writing a digraph (two letters) they should say **one sound**.  This will fix these patterns in memory.

**Reading from the Storybook**.  **Be sure to read the entire story for the lesson from the Storybook on the same day as the lesson**.  Read at a quiet time, after a snack, before a nap or bedtime, *or any time the child asks*.  The stories reinforce the target sound the child is learning about.

**Creative Writing**.  Encourage creative writing.  This increases the child's ability to write connected prose and to try out some poetry.  It is an excellent diagnostic tool for you.  As before, incorrect but 'possible' spellings are OK.  Impossible spellings are not OK.  Use the child's spelling errors to clear up any confusion.

**Introducing Digraphs.**  Before you begin teaching the first digraph (**sh**), tell children this true story in words they can understand:

> *A long time ago there was no way to write words, and there were no books written in English.  The King of England and priests from the the church decided to borrow the letters from the Roman alphabet for their new writing system, but there were only enough letters for half the sounds in the English language.  When they ran out of letters, what do you think they did then?  They could have made up some new letters, but they didn't.  This would have made it a lot easier to learn to read and spell.  Instead, they put two of the old letters side-by-side to stand for the left-over sounds.  There are lots of letter pairs that stand for only one sound.*

This story makes the additional point that a writing system is an invention.  The *sounds* in our language are the important thing.  Arbitrary letters are assigned to *real* sounds.  And this is why children must absolutely understand that ***the sounds in our language are the basis for the code,*** and not the letters themselves.

## the sound /k/      Kind King Karl

Read the story for enjoyment.  Do the listening exercise.  Read the story again and ask the child to listen for the sound **/k/.**  Say **/k/** and a puff of air.  Don't say 'kay' or 'kuh'.

King Karl lived in Crickle-Rock Castle,
on the crest of a hill in the Kingdom of Crickle.
It looked out over Crickle Lake.
You could see the cliffs of Crickle on a clear day.

King Karl wasn't very kingly.
He didn't like people in crowds or singly.
He kept to his castle far from town.
He never, ever wore his crown.

He liked a good book.
He liked Kate his cook.
He liked good food when he dined,
but mainly he liked animals of any kind.

---

### Listening for the Sound /k/

**Read each sentence below to the child.**

The sound you hear the most in this story is /**k**/.  [Say 'k' and a puff of air.]

Watch my mouth when I say this sound:  /**k**/  [open your mouth wide]

Now you say the sound /**k**/.  Say the word '**king**' and listen for the sound /**k**/.

Is it the first or the last sound?

Say the word '**duck**' and listen for the sound /**k**/.  Is it the first or the last sound?

When I say the word '**racket**' hold up your hand when you hear the sound /**k**/.  I'm going to say each sound slowly:

      **r---a---ck---e---t**

Now you push the sounds together to make the word.

Here's a really hard one:  Listen while I say the sounds slowly.  How many /**k**/ sounds do you hear?

      **p---i---c---n---i---c**

Now let's see if you can push the sounds together to make the word.

If the child needs extra practice, do more words with /**k**/.  Reread the story and do the listening exercise.   Do the **Write It, Say It** exercises for the sound /**k**/.

# Write It, Say It

Tell the child: "There are three ways to write the sound **/k/**." Do this in three separate exercises. Have the child trace the letter **k**, then copy it below and on lined paper, then write it from memory, saying the sound **/k/** each time. Repeat with the letter **c**, then with the letters **ck**. Tell the child that the letters **ck** stand for only one sound.

# K

k     k     k     k     k     k

---

# C

c     c     c     c     c     c

---

# CK

ck     ck     ck     ck     ck     ck

---

## the sound /k/     Word Fun

SAY: "In these words the sound **/k/** is the first sound in the word. There are two ways to spell it." **Do the copying and spelling activities** (see Instructions on page 3 for this section.).

# c and k

| | |
|---|---|
| c---a---b | cab |
| c---a---n | can |
| c---a---p | cap |
| c---a---t | cat |
| c---o---t | cot |
| c---u---b | cub |
| c---u---p | cup |
| c---u---t | cut |
| c---u---ff | cuff |
| k---e---g | keg |
| k---i---d | kid |
| k---i---t | kit |
| k---i---ss | kiss |
| K---e---n | Ken |

## the sound /k/    Word Fun

SAY: "*The sound /k/ is the last sound in these words. It is spelled with two letters, but only has one /k/ sound. This spelling [point to **ck**] comes at the end of words and never at the beginning.*" **Do the copying and spelling exercises.**

# ck

| | | | |
|---|---|---|---|
| s---a---ck | sack | n---e---ck | neck |
| c---o---ck | cock | l---o---ck | lock |
| r---o---ck | rock | k---i---ck | kick |
| s---o---ck | sock | d---u---ck | duck |

| | |
|---|---|
| back | pack |
| peck | tack |
| deck | dock |
| luck | lick |
| sick | suck |
| tuck | pick |
| tick | tock |
| Jack | Nick |
| Jock | Vicky |
| | SAY: This says Vickee |

the sound /k/        **Word Fun**

## Four-sound words

SAY: *"These words have four sounds. In the first group of words the sound /k/ is the first sound. It can be spelled two ways."* **Do the copying and spelling exercises when both sets are done**.

# c    and    k

| | | | |
|---|---|---|---|
| c---l---a---p | clap | c---l---a---m | clam |
| c---l---i---ff | cliff | c---r---a---b | crab |
| c---r---i---b | crib | c---a---m---p | camp |
| k---i---l---t | kilt | | |

| | | |
|---|---|---|
| class | clip | cross |
| club | crop | can't |
| cast | cost | kept |

SAY: *"In these words, the sound /k/ is the second sound in the word.*

| | | | |
|---|---|---|---|
| S---c---o---t | Scot | s---k---i---d | skid |
| s---k---i---p | skip | s---k---i---ff | skiff |

| | | |
|---|---|---|
| scan | scat | skin |
| scuff | skim | skill |
| across | | |

**Help with 'across.' It has two syllables: uh-cross'**

## the sound /k/
## Four-sound Words ending /k/

SAY: *"These words have four sounds. The sound **/k/** is the last sound. When the sound **/k/** comes at the ends of words, you can write it two ways."* **Do the copying and spelling exercises.**

# ck

| | | | |
|---|---|---|---|
| b---l---a---ck | black | b---r---i---ck | brick |
| s---t---i---ck | stick | b---l---o---ck | block |
| c---l---o---ck | clock | t---r---u---ck | truck |

| | | |
|---|---|---|
| crack | flock | trick |
| stack | track | smock |
| trick | smock | stuck |

# k

| | | | |
|---|---|---|---|
| m---i---l---k | milk | m---a---s---k | mask |
| t---u---s---k | tusk | d---e---s---k | desk |

| | | |
|---|---|---|
| ask | task | sulk |
| silk | risk | dusk |

**Special Words below: SAY:** *"These words are spelled funny. People used to say these words like they are written but not any more."*

| | |
|---|---|
| t---a---(l)---k | **talk** (tok) |
| w---a---(l)---k | **walk** (wok) |

# Really Reading

## Reading words with the sound /k/

Ken has a black cat.  His cat got sick.

His cat can't walk.

A vet can help Ken's cat get well.

When Ken got his cat back, his cat was well.

Ken was glad.  Ken's cat got a big hug.


Nick dug clams in soft sand.

A crab ran at Nick.

A crab was fast and bit Nick.

A crab bit Nick on his hand.

Nick's skin got red.

Nick was cross.


## *Jack Got Lost in Scotland*

Jack went on a walk up a hill in Scotland.

He had a back-pack.

Jack will camp in a tent.

Jack had bad luck.

His tent fell in a gust of wind.

Jack had to get back, but he got lost.

Jack met Jock.  Jock was a Scot.  Jock had on a kilt.

Jack and Jock had a talk.

Jock has a truck.  He can help Jack get back.

Jack got back at ten o'clock.

# More ways to spell the sound /k/

*Reading and spelling words with the sounds 'kw'*

[**This is the last Write It, Say It exercise**.]  SAY: "**The sounds  '/k/ +  /w/** [say "kw" and a puff of air.  Don't say: 'kwuh'] *are always spelled like this*." [point to <u>qu</u> ].

# qu

Children should read the words below, then copy **qu** several times on lined paper, saying '**kw**' each time it is written.  Be sure the tail of the **q** hangs below the line.

**Don't forget spelling dictation.  Include all the /k/ spellings in your choice of words.**

qu---i---t                quit

qu---a---ck               quack

qu---i---ck               quick

qu---i---z                quiz

qu---i---l---t            quilt

qu---e---s---t            quest

# More Ways to Spell the Sound /k/

**Words ending with the sounds 'ks'.**

SAY: *"This letter stands for two sounds: 'ks'. It is the only letter that stands for two sounds."* The <u>x</u> is easy to write, so do copying and spelling exercises only. As the child writes <u>x</u>, make sure he says *two sounds*: *'/k/-/s/'*.

# X

| | |
|---|---|
| a---x | ax |
| s---a---x | sax |
| o---x | ox |
| b---o---x | box |
| f---o---x | fox |
| t---u---x | tux |

| | |
|---|---|
| fax | wax |
| fix | mix |
| six | next |
| Max | exit |

# Really Reading

Reading words with the sounds /k/ and /ks/.  All /k/ spellings included.

## *Huck the Duck*

Huck was a duck
Huck swam on a pond
Huck went quack, quack.
Huck can swim fast.
Huck is quick.

## *Six Fox Cubs Had a Walk*

A fox kept six cubs in a den.
Six cubs got fat and big.
A fox and six cubs went off on a walk.
A fox and six cubs went past
     Huck and two ducks on a pond,
     Jack on a hill,
     Max, an ox,
     a cock in a pen,
     and a cat in a box.

A fox and six cubs went back.
A fox and six cubs went past
     a cat in a box,
     a cock in a pen,
     Max, an ox,
     Jack on a hill
     Huck and two ducks on a pond.

A fox and six cubs got back at dusk.
Next, six cubs had a rest.

## the sound /sh/          The Silver Shadow

Read this story for enjoyment.  Do the listening exercise.  Read the story again and ask the child to listen for the sound **/sh/**.  Do Word Fun and the copying and spelling activities.

In the fishing village of Ashton-on-Sea,
Mr. Shaw worked on his invention.
He was building a new kind of sailing ship
That one man could sail alone on the ocean.

He called her the 'Silver Shadow.'
It had a mast of sheer, shiny metal
with a very special shape
that was thin and incredibly tall.

Now the Shadow needed a test.
Mr. Shaw put her in a competition
with the other ships in her class.
It was a race on the open ocean.

---

### Listening for the Sound /sh/

**Read each sentence below to the child.**

The sound you hear the most in this story is **/sh/**.

Watch my mouth when I say this sound **/sh/**.  When I say the word **'shadow'** listen for the sound **/sh/**.  Is it the first or the last sound?

When I say the word **'fish'** listen for the sound **/sh/**.  Is it the first or the last sound?

Listen when I say this word.  Put up your hand when I say the sound **/sh/**.

   **finish**

Now I'm going to say a word slowly.  Put up your hand when I say the sound **/sh/**.

   **o---sh---u---n**  (o*ce*an).

Now you push these sound together to make the word.

If the child needs extra practice, then do more words with **/sh/**.  Reread the story and do the listening game.  Do Word Fun next.

## the sound   /sh/        Word Fun

Tell the story in the Introduction to this section.  SAY:  "The sound **/sh/** is written with two letters."  **Do the copying and spelling exercises**.

| | | | |
|---|---|---|---|
| sh---i---n | shin | sh---i---p | ship |
| sh---e---d | shed | sh---e---ll | shell |
| sh---o---p | shop | Sh---e---p | Shep |

|  |  |
|---|---|
| shot | shut |
| shack | shock |

## Special word:       she
  Say: 'this word is    shee'

| | | | |
|---|---|---|---|
| c---a---sh | cash | m---a---sh | mash |
| r---a---sh | rash | d---i---sh | dish |
| f---i---sh | fish | s---a---sh | sash |

|  |  |
|---|---|
| ash | dash |
| gash | hash |
| wish | gush |
| hush | lush |
| rush | gosh |

# the sound /sh/

## Four and five sound words.

SAY: *"Here are some longer words with /sh/."*  **Do the copying and spelling exercises.**

sh---e---l---f          shelf

sh---r---e---d          shred

c---r---a---sh          crash

f---l---a---sh          flash

s---m---a---sh          smash

b---r---u---sh          brush

sh---r---i---m---p      shrimp

s---p---l---a---sh      splash

| | |
|---|---|
| shift | shrill |
| clash | stash |
| slash | flesh |
| plush | blush |
| crush | slush |
| slosh | swish |
| fresh | Welsh |

# Really Reading

## Reading words with the sound /sh/

Jill got a clam in the soft sand.
It was shut.
She got a big shell as well.


Nick and his dog Shep
went on his skiff in a fresh wind.
His skiff went fast.
He felt a splash on his skin.
Nick can fish from his skiff.
Nick got a big fish.
He can land his fish himself.
Mom will fix Nick's fish.


## *Jack Walsh and his Cash*

[Help children read the word 'bank.']

Jack Walsh shut up his shop.
He kept his cash in a jug on a shelf.
Jack got his trash in a box in a shed, and he left.

A bad man did smash a lock on Jack's shop.
A bad man got Jack's cash in a jug on a shelf.
A bad man did rush off, quick as a flash.
But a cop got him.

Jack Walsh had a shock.
Gosh!  He must get his cash in a bank quick.

## the sound /oo/          Mrs. Hood's Pudding

This is a new vowel sound.  Read the story for enjoyment.  Do the listening exercise.  Read the story again and ask the child to listen for the sound **/oo/.**  Don't confuse the sound **/oo/** (*book)* with the sound  **/oo/** (*food)*.  [**Watch out**.  The sound /oo/ can be spelled **u** as in '*pudding*.'.]

Emma Hood was fond of food.
She liked to cook
from a tall cook book
with 96 ways to make puddings.

One day she looked
and she was hooked.
On page 43, there it stood.
It sounded ever so good:

*"Full cream fudge-nut pudding"*

---

### Listening for the Sound /oo/

**Read each sentence below to the child.**

The sound you hear the most in this story is /**oo**/.  [keep it short]

Watch my mouth when I say this sound:  /**oo**/  [lips rounded and pushed forward]

It's like a monkey noise, isn't it?  Now you say /**oo**/.

Say the word '**book**' and listen for the sound /**oo**/.  It's the middle sound.

Say the word '**push**' and listen for the sound /**oo**/.  It's the middle sound again, isn't it?

Now I'm going to say some sounds slowly.  Raise your hand when you hear the sound /**oo**/.

      **p---u---dd---i---ng**

Now you push the sounds together to make the word.

--------------------------------------------------------------------------------------------
If children need extra practice, do more words with /**oo**/.  Reread the story and play the listening game.  Go on to Word Fun.

## the sound /oo/     Word Fun

SAY: *"The sound /oo/ is spelled with double letters."* **Do the copying and spelling exercises.**

| | |
|---|---|
| b---oo---k | book |
| h---oo---k | hook |
| f---oo---t | foot |
| w---oo---d | wood |
| c---oo---k | cook |
| b---r---oo---k | brook |

| | |
|---|---|
| took | nook |
| good | look |
| hoof | soot |
| hood | woof |
| roof | stood |
| crook | shook |

**Another**   **put**     **pull**     **full**     **push**
**spelling**
SAY: the sound **/oo/** is spelled **u** (point to **u** ) in these words.

**Special words:**     **could**    **should**    **would**
SAY, these words are:     cood     shood     wood

Tell children: *"These words are spelled funny. You will have to memorize them."* [These are the only words spelled like this.]

# Really Reading
### Reading words with the sound /oo/

## *Max Was a Bad Pup*

Max is a pup.
Max has lots of pep.

Max ran off and fell in a brook.
Max shook himself off on Sally Crook.

Max got up on Mom's cookbook.
Mom's book got wet and she can't cook.

Max ran in mud and soot.
Max stood on Dad's foot.

Max took off in the woods.
Max would not be good.

Dad put Max in a full tub.
Max got a good scrub.

Dad will fix Max on a hook.
Max has a sad look.

Max could jump, and Max could pull.
But Max can't run off.
Max went, "Woof, woof, woof."

# the sound /oo/    The New Sign at the Pool

Read the story for enjoyment.  Do the listening exercise.  Read the story again and ask the child to listen for the sound /oo/.  Go to Word Fun.  [Teachers:  Put this sign on the board—put a line around it, and read it to the children.]

**This pool is for the use**
**of the loon and the goose.**
**KEEP OUT**

| | |
|---|---|
| **Moose** | **Poodle** |
| **Raccoon** | **Kangaroo** |
| **Rooster** | **Cat** |

There was something new
In the park by the pool.
it was white and blue.
It was wood, that's a clue.

Mooly Moose came over to see.
"Hmmm.  It's wood.  It's not a stool.
Well, well, you've got me.
Gee, I must be a fool.
Hey, it says 'moo,'" said he.

---

**Listening for the Sound /oo/**

**Read each sentence below to the child.**

The sound you hear the most in this story is /oo/.  Watch my mouth when I say this sound: /oo/  [make a small round shape]

Now you say the sound /oo/.  Say the word '**moon**' and listen for the sound /oo/.  It comes in the middle, doesn't it?

Say the word '**zoo**' and listen for the sound /oo/.  Is it the first or the last sound?

Listen while I say this word.  Raise your hand when you hear the sound /oo/.

> **school**

Now I'm going to say another word slowly.   **b---l---oo**  (blue).  Push the sounds together to make the word.

If necessary, do more /oo/ words.  Read the story and play the listening game.  Go to Word Fun.  Tell child to notice that this is the same spelling as for /oo/ in 'book.'

## the sound /<u>oo</u>/     Word Fun

Tell children that this is the same spelling as the last sound, but it stands for <u>/oo/</u> (a different sound) in these words. **Do the copying and spelling exercises.**

| | |
|---|---|
| z---oo | zoo |
| m---oo---n | moon |
| b---oo---t | boot |
| h---oo---p | hoop |
| p---oo---l | pool |
| f---oo---d | food |
| c---oo---p | coop |
| s---c---oo---p | scoop |
| b—r---oo---m | broom |
| s---t---oo---l | stool |
| s---p---oo---n | spoon |

| | | |
|---|---|---|
| moo | boo | too |
| toot | noon | mood |
| boom | hoot | zoom |
| loop | fool | soon |
| cool | groom | troop |
| droop | stoop | snoopy |

**Special words:**   **to**    **too**    **two**    **do**    **blue**    **moose**    **goose**    **loose**
Say, these are: too   too    too    doo    bloo    moos    goos    loos
Define the first 3 words.

## Mooly Moose Got Loose

Ned and Sally went to the zoo at noon.
Mom and Dad went too.
They had food at the zoo.
The zoo is fun.  The zoo has lots to do.


At two o'clock Mooly Moose got loose.
Mooly Moose went in a blue pool.
He went in to get cool.
The ducks and loons and a goose swam in the blue pool too.


Mooly Moose left the blue pool and went off to beg food.
He went up to Ned and Sally.
Sally fed him a bun.  Ned fed him a hot dog.
Sally was glad she met a moose.
She was glad he was in a good mood,
and she could pet him too.


Two men from the zoo
had to get Mooly Moose back.
Two men led him back soon.
Two men had to brush and groom him.
Mooly Moose got a big hug from two men.
Mooly Moose got lots of food.

## the sound /th/     How Queen Beth Lost Her Throne

Read the story and do the listening exercise.  Read the story again and ask children to listen for the sound **/th/** [tongue between your teeth]   There are two sounds spelled the same way; one is voiced (**them**) and one unvoiced (**thing).**  Go to Word Fun.

Princess Beth was born in the Kingdom of Thring.
One day she would be the Queen.
But this happened far too soon.
Poor Beth seemed to be doomed.

Her mother died at her birth.
Then one day, her father was thrown from his horse.
He said this to Beth with his dying breath,
      "Remember this –
      Love and kindness are worth more than wealth.
      Don't trust my brother Ethelrood.
      He's a thief through and through.
      Flee to the north or the south.
      Go anywhere on this earth.
      You must get away from the Kingdom of Thring."

But Beth was still in her youth.
She couldn't flee to the north or the south.
There was nothing she could do.

---

### Listening for the Sound /th/

**Read each sentence below to the child.**

The sound you heard the most in this story is **/th/.**  [unvoiced—'thin']

Watch my mouth when I say this sound: **/th/**  [tongue between teeth—blow air]

Now you say the sound **/th/.**   Tell me if the sound **/th/** comes first or last in these words:

    **thin**            **bath**            **broth**          **thank**

In some words this sound is "buzzy" or "noisy".  Listen:  **th---e---m**    **them**    [tongue between teeth+buzz of voicing]

Can you hear this sound is 'buzzy'?  Say the word **'them'** and listen for the sound **'th'.**

Say the word **'smooth'** and listen for the sound **'th'.**   Listen while I say a word slowly.
Raise your hand when you hear the sound **'th'.**        **m---o---th---er**

You push the sounds together and say the word.

------------------------------------------------------------------------------------------------

Practice if necessary.  Reread the story and do the listening game.  Go to Word Fun.

# the sound  /th/  Word Fun

Make it clear which **/th/** sounds are voiced and which unvoiced.  Do the copying and spelling exercises.

## /th/ is fuzzy (unvoiced) in these words:

| | | | |
|---|---|---|---|
| m---o---th | moth | b---a---th | bath |
| p---a---th | path | t---oo---th | tooth |
| b---oo---th | booth | c---l---o---th | cloth |
| f---r---o---th | froth | b---r---o---th | broth |
| B---e---th | Beth | C—a—th—y | Cathy |

| | | |
|---|---|---|
| thin | thick | with |
| thud | thrill | depth |

## /th/ is buzzy (voiced) in these words:

| | | | |
|---|---|---|---|
| th---a---n | than | th---a---t | that |
| th---i---s | this | th---e---n | then |
| th---e---m | them | s---m---oo---th | smooth |

Help with these words:

| | | | |
|---|---|---|---|
| f---a---th---er | father | m---o---th---er | mother |
| b---r---o---th---er | brother | | |

**Special word:**    they
This word says:    thay

# Really Reading
### Reading words with the sound /th/

Help with unfamiliar words like  'go'  'lather'  'happy'  'water.'

## *The Brothers*

This is the story of Mick and his brother Ben.
Mick is bigger than Ben.
Mick is too big, but then,
Ben is too thin.

The kids call them
Mick Thick and Ben Thin.

When Mick walks across the room,
his steps go thud, thump, thud.
His mother says, "Sh."
His father says, "Hush."
But Mick cannot help it.

Ben walks with a soft, quick step.
Ben's steps go tip-tap, tip-tap, tip-tap.
His mother and father do not say,
"Sh"  or "Hush."
They can't tell when Ben is in.

Mick and Ben went on a walk.
They went on a path up a hill.
Ben was swift.  Ben was quick.
Ben soon got to the top.

Mick could not go fast.
Mick went thud, thud, thud.
Mick went huff and puff.
Mick was last to get to the top.
Then Mick fell with a thump.

Ben gets into his bath with no splash.
The water is smooth and still.
It does not spill.

Ben has a duck and a swan in the bath.
Ben has a wash with his wash cloth.
He lathers up with a good froth.

When Mick gets into the bath,
it goes swoosh, and splish, and splash.
It fills to the top.
Oops!

It begins to spill.
Drip, drop, drip, drop ----
Onto the bath mat, into the bathroom, into the hall.
Mom and Dad are not happy at all.

## the sound /ng/    King Ching Meets King Kong

Read the story.  Do the listening exercise.  Read the story again and ask children to listen to the sound **/ng/**.  Make this sound by pushing the back of your tongue against your teeth.  Play the listening game.  [The spelling **nk** stands for the sounds **/ng/-/k/.**]

This is a story about a famous King
Who lived in China a long time ago.
His name was King Ching.
He was King of all Ming.
King Ching was a very rich king.
He wore ten gold rings,
one for every royal finger.

King Ching was too young to be king.
He was selfish and mean.
He had a big gong that he never left for long.
When his servants heard bong-bong-bong
they knew they would have to bring
almost anything.

---

### Listening for the Sound /ng/

**Read each sentence below to the child.**

The sound you heard the most in this story is **/ng/**

Watch my mouth when I say this sound: **/ng/** [open your mouth wide]
Now you say the sound **/ng/**

The sound **/ng/** comes at the ends or the middle of words, but never at the beginning.
Raise your hand when you hear the sound **/ng/** in these words:

**ring          hang          song          sting**

This sound can come in the middle of words.  Listen while I say this word slowly:

**j---u---ng---u---l**   (jungle)

Now you push the sounds together to make the word.
-----------------------------------------------------------------------------------------
If your child needs extra practice, do more words with /ng/.  Reread the story and do the listening game.  Go to Word Fun.

## the sound /ng/        Word Fun

Notice that the words at the top have three sounds, and the words at the bottom have four and five sounds. **Do the copying and spelling exercises.**

## 3 sound words

| g---a---ng | gang | | r---i---ng | ring |
|---|---|---|---|---|
| k---i---ng | king | | s---o---ng | song |

p---i---ng   p---o---ng      ping-pong

| | |
|---|---|
| bang | fang |
| rang | sang |
| sing | thing |
| long | song |
| hung | sung |

## 4 and 5 sound words

| a---l---o---ng | along | b---r---i---ng bring |
|---|---|---|
| f---l---i---ng | fling | c---l---i---ng cling |
| s---t---r---o---ng | strong | s---t---r---i---ng    string |
| s---p---r---i---ng | spring | |

| Special | E---ng---l---i---sh | English |
|---|---|---|
| *Words :* | *E---ng---l---a--n---d* | *England* |

120

# the sounds /ng/-/k/

Note: the sound **/ng/** is spelled **n** in words ending in the sounds **/ng/-/k/** and **only in these words**. Tell the child that **n** stands for **/ng/** in these words. **Do the copying and writing exercises.**

| | | | |
|---|---|---|---|
| t---a---ng---k | tank | r---i---ng---k | rink |
| b---u---ng---k | bunk | j---u---ng---k | junk |
| s---k---u---ng---k  skunk | | t---r---ng---k | trunk |

## Practice Words

| | |
|---|---|
| bank | tank |
| sank | sunk |
| honk | wink |
| think | thank |
| drink | drank |
| blink | pink |
| stink | stank |

## Adding 'ing' to make a new word:

Copy the words below onto a piece of paper. Tell the child to add the letters: **ing** and then read the word. Tell her that the word-ending **'ing'** means "doing something now."

| | | | |
|---|---|---|---|
| bang | hang | ring | sing |
| long | bring | sting | cling |
| fling | string | spring | blink |
| bank | thank | wink | honk |
| think | sink | drink | |

# Really Reading

Reading words with the sound **/ng/**.  Cover the lines below where the child is reading.

## The King's Long Song

A big bell rang.

A big gong went bong.

The king had a wish to sing.

The king will sing a song.

The king sang on and on.

The song was too long.

The song did not stop.

Someone said, "We wish he will quit.

The king can't sing a thing."

But the king kept on singing.

## A Tank Sank

A tank went too fast.     Zoom!

It ran into a bank of mud.     Boom!     Smash!

The tank slid off the bank and fell in a pond.     Splash!

The tank began sinking.     Slosh!

The tank sank, quick as a wink.     Swoosh!

A gang of men had to bring it up.     Grunt!

They took weeks and weeks.   Gosh!

It took too long.

The tank was bent.

It had a big dent.

It had a gash.

It had a lot of rust.

The tank was a mess.

The gang of men had to quit.

The gang of men left the tank on a bank.


The tank is just rusting junk.

## the sound  /ch/        The Fate of the Water Witch
**Two spellings for /ch/:  <u>ch</u>  <u>tch</u>**

Read the story.  Do the listening exercise.  Read the story again and play the listening game.  Go to Word Fun.

Captain Richard and his chief mate Mitch
stood on the deck of the Water Witch.
The Witch was a two-masted ketch.
It was a pirate ship which no one could catch.

They were looking for gold to snatch.
They stole from the ships of the Dutch and French.
The Witch roamed the English channel,
And Richard charted each ship in his journal.

---

### Listening for the Sound /ch/

**Read each sentence below to the child.**

The sound you hear the most in this story is /**ch**/.

Watch my mouth when I say this sound: /**ch**/  [lips forward, short, sharp push of air]

Now you say the sound /**ch**/.

Listen while I say these words.  You say whether /**ch**/ is the first or the last sound.

| | |
|---|---|
| **rich** | **bunch** |
| **chum** | **watch** |
| **chase** | **chest** |

Now listen while I say these sounds slowly, and raise your hand when you hear the sound /**ch**/.

**R---i---ch---ar---d**

Push the sounds together to say this word.

-------------------------------------------------------------------------------------------

If necessary, do more words with /**ch**/.  Reread the story and do the listening game.  Go to Word Fun.

**the sound  /ch/          Word Fun**

NOTE:  On this page the sound /ch/ is spelled <u>ch</u>.  This spelling can come in any position in a word.  On the next page, the spelling is <u>tch</u>.  **Do the copying and spelling activities for each spelling separately.**

# ch

| | | | |
|---|---|---|---|
| ch---i---n | chin | ch---o---p | chop |
| ch---e---ss | chess | ch---i---ck | chick |
| ch---e---s---t | chest | ch---i---ck---e---n | chicken |
| ch---i---p---s | chips | ch---i---m---p | chimp |
| p---oo---ch | pooch | l---u---n---ch | lunch |

| | | |
|---|---|---|
| chat | chap | chum |
| check | inch | much |
| rich | such | bench |
| bunch | hunch | pinch |
| punch | branch | crunch |
| drench | French | trench |

125

**the sound /ch/**      **Word Fun**

SAY: "There is another way to spell the sound **/ch/** (point). This spelling happens at the ends of words and never at the beginning." **Do the copying and spelling exercises.**

# tch

| | | | |
|---|---|---|---|
| i---tch | itch | c---a---tch | catch |
| f---e---tch | fetch | m---a---tch | match |
| th---a---tch | thatch | w---a---tch | watch* |
| p---a---tch | patch | w---i---tch | witch |
| p---i---tch | pitch | d---i---tch | ditch |
| D---u---tch | Dutch | | |

| | |
|---|---|
| s---k---e---tch | sketch |
| s---n---a---tch | snatch |
| s---w---i---tch | switch |
| s---c---r---a---tch | scratch |
| s---t---r---e---tch | stretch |

* the **wa** spelling usually sounds: 'waw'

# Really Reading
### Reading words with the sound /ch/

## *The Missing Chimp*

A troop of chimps was in a zoo.

One chimp ran off from the zoo.


A man went to fetch him.

The chimp was sitting on a patch of grass.

He had a big branch in his fist.

He began to hoot and thump his chest.

The chimp was much too big and strong.

One man could not catch him.


Six men went to fetch him.

Six men took a lot of food.

It did no good.

The chimp will not get up from the patch of grass.

He would not drop his branch.

Six men could not catch him.


A bunch of men went to fetch him.

The chimp was not a match for a bunch of men.

The chimp was quick to get up off the grass.

His left his branch on the patch of grass.

They took the chimp back to the zoo.

He had his lunch with the troop.

# Special Section

## on

# Alternative Spellings

## for the Sounds

/n/   /w/   /r/   /j/   /s/   /v/   /u/   /e/   /<u>oo</u>/

# Parents/Teachers

So far children have learned the main spelling for each sound that has been taught. They have also learned spelling alternatives for **/k/** **/ng/** and **/ch/**. All but one of the remaining sounds have spelling alternatives. This section presents the common spelling alternatives for the sounds children **have learned so far.**

No sounds in the language have a perfect one-to-one correspondence between sound and letter symbol(s). But many come close. These sounds mainly have one spelling are in the order in which they were introduced:

**p t m a d i g b h l th ng**   and the sound pair /**kw**/ (**qu**)

The spellings of some sounds are predicted by whether they come first or last in a word:
**v/ve      j/dge** or **ge   ch/ch** or **tch**

Spelling alternatives for the following sounds are taught in this section:
**n      w      r      s      j      v      u      e      oo**

The suffix **/er/** (a vowel sound)  is introduced here also. It greatly expands reading vocabulary. This is a different sound to the consonant **/r/**. The vowel **/er/** varies with dialect. In some dialects, it becomes '**eh**' or '**uh**'. The child should read **er** in his dialect.

The lessons that follow are intended to familiarize the child with common spelling alternatives for sounds he already knows, and to make the important point that many sounds have more than one spelling. These lessons may not be sufficient to anchor the new spellings in memory. As you continue in the program, these spellings will appear in many new words. Remind your child about them. **If necessary, return to these lessons and teach them again.**

## Instructions

**Word Fun**. Every word is segmented so the child can **see** which letters work together and which do not. Do this exercise in the usual way. Take time to insure that the final reading of each word is fluent and at the normal rate. Be sure to **do the copying and writing activities with each page**. Children must say each sound out loud as it is written. **Really Reading**. One story includes all the sounds taught in this section and their various spelling alternatives. It is optional, and may be too difficult right now.

Begin each lesson with this information:  **"You know the main way to write this sound. This sound has more than one spelling. We're going to learn a new spelling for this sound."**

# Word Fun
## New spellings for consonants that begin words

SAY: *"You know the main way to spell these sounds. Here are some other ways to spell them."*
**You must do the copying and spelling exercises after each sound.**

## the sound /n/   <u>**kn**</u>

kn---i---t      knit        kn---o---t      knot        kn---o---ck      knock

## the sound /r/   <u>**wr**</u>

wr---a---p      wrap            wr---e---n      wren

wr---e---ck     wreck           wr---i---ng     wring

wr---o---ng     wrong           wr---i---s---t  wrist

## the sound  /w/   <u>**wh**</u>

wh---e---n      when            wh---i---p      whip

wh---i---ch     which           wh---i---s---k  whisk

**Special words:**              what            who
   SAY,  this word is          wut             hoo

## the sound /s/      <u>**c**</u>

c---e---ll      cell                c---e---n---t      cent

c---i---t---y   city                c---i---n---ch     cinch

130

# Word Fun
## New spellings for sounds that end words

## the sound /j/

SAY: *"You know how to write the sound /j/ at the beginning of words. This sound is spelled differently at the ends of words. It is spelled two ways:"* point to **dge** and **ge.**
**Do the copying and spelling exercises.**

## dge

| | | | |
|---|---|---|---|
| e---dge | edge | b---a---dge | badge |
| b---u---dge | budge | f---u---dge | fudge |
| h---e---dge | hedge | j---u---dge | judge |
| l---e---dge | ledge | l---o---dge | lodge |
| r---i---dge | ridge | w---e---dge | wedge |
| d---o---dge | dodge | n---u---dge | nudge |
| b---r---i---dge | bridge | f---r---i---dge | fridge |
| s---m---u---dge | smudge | t---r---u---dge | trudge |

## ge

[WATCH OUT: **n g** does not combine to stand for one sound in these words].

| | | | |
|---|---|---|---|
| h---i---n---ge | hinge | b---u---l---ge | bulge |
| f---r---i---n---ge | fringe | p---l---u---n---ge | plunge |

# Word Fun
## New spellings for sounds that end words

## the sound /s/

SAY: *"The sound /s/ has a lot of different spellings. You know the two main ways."* Write **s** and **ss** on paper or board. *"Here are two more ways to spell this sound. These spellings come at the ends of words."* **Do the copying and spelling exercises.**

## ce

| | | | |
|---|---|---|---|
| d---a---n---ce | dance | f---e---n---ce | fence |
| s---i---n---ce | since | m---i---n---ce | mince |
| g---l---a---n---ce | glance | p---r---i---n---ce | prince |
| p---r---a---n---ce | prance | F---r---a---n---ce | France |

**Special word:**
Say, this says

once
'wunce'

## se

| | | | |
|---|---|---|---|
| g---oo---se | goose | m---oo---se | moose |
| l---oo---se | loose | n---oo---se | noose |
| d--e---n---se | dense | r---i---n---se | rinse |
| s---e---n---se | sense | t---e---n---se | tense |

---

## the sound /v/

SAY: *"The sound **/v/** is **always** written like this (point) at the ends of words."*

## ve

| | | | |
|---|---|---|---|
| g---i---ve | give | l---i---ve | live |
| h---a---ve | have | | |

132

# Word Fun
## New spellings for vowels

## the sound /u/

SAY: *"You know the main way to write the sound /u/ (fun). Here is another way to spell it. This is the same spelling we use for the sound /o/ in 'hot.' So this is tricky."* **Do the copying and spelling activities**.

## O

l---o---ve      love         g---l---o---ve      glove

sh---o---ve      shove       a---b---o---ve      above

SAY: This word is 'uh-buv'

s---o---n      son          w---o---n      won

f---r---o---n---t      front       m---o---n---th      month

n---o---th---i---ng      nothing

c---o---me      come        d---o---ne      done

n---o---ne      none         s---o---me      some

SAY: *The last sound is /er/ in these words.*

o---th---er      other        b---r---o---th---er      brother

m---o---th---er      mother      a---n---o---th---er      another

**Special words.**      does       once
  Say, these words are:     duz        wunce

# Word Fun
## New spellings for vowels

## The sound /e/

SAY: *"You know the main way to spell the sound /e/ (bed). Here's another way."*
[point]. **Do the copying and spelling activities.**

# ea

| | | | |
|---|---|---|---|
| b---r---ea---d | bread | b---r---ea---th | breath |
| d---ea---d | dead | d---ea---th | death |
| d---ea---f | deaf | h---ea---d | head |
| h---ea---l---th | health | m---ea---n---t | meant |
| th---r---ea---d | thread | w---ea---l---th | wealth |
| i---n---s---t---ea---d | instead | | |

**Words ending with /er/**

| | | | |
|---|---|---|---|
| f---ea---th---er | feather | l---ea---th---er | leather |
| h---ea---th---er | heather | w---ea---th---er | weather |

| **Special words:** | **said** | **again** | **friend** |
|---|---|---|---|
| Say, these words are: | sed | uh-gen | frend |

## the sound /oo/     Word Fun

SAY: *"You know the main way to write the sound /**oo**/.  Here are some new ways."* **Do the copying and spelling exercises**.

# ue

| | | | |
|---|---|---|---|
| b---l---ue | blue | c---l---ue | clue |
| g---l---ue | glue | t---r---ue | true |

SAY: "In the these words the letters **u** and **e** are split apart but still work together to stand for the sound **oo**."

# u-e

| | | | |
|---|---|---|---|
| f---l---u---t-e | flute | J---u---n-e | June |
| r---u---d-e | rude | r---u---l-e | rule |

# ew

| | | | |
|---|---|---|---|
| n---ew | new | d---ew | dew |
| b---l---ew | blew | ch---ew | chew |
| c---r---ew | crew | d---r---ew | drew |
| f---l---ew | flew | g---r---ew | grew |
| s---t---ew | stew | kn---ew | knew |
| th---r---ew | threw | | |

**Special words:**  f--r--ui--t  fruit  j--ui--ce  juice
Say, these words are:  froot  joos

[Watch your dialect. **new, dew, stew, knew** are pronounced '**ee-oo**' in the UK.]

135

# Really Reading

## New Spellings for Old Sounds

**This story is optional.** If children did well on the preceding lessons, they can read this story. If they were struggling, repeat the previous lessons and come back to this later. Help with the new words: **said, kitchen, hello, I, tummy**. Explain what the quotation marks and question marks mean. Tell the child what a **hedgehog** is. If possible find a picture of one.

## *Hodge Podge the Hedgehog*

Hodge Podge lives with his mom in a hedge.

They live on a hill in France.

Once he went on a long walk in the month of June.

He went on the grass, then on a path past a fence.

He went across a bridge, into a ditch, and up a hill.

He got to a big lodge on the edge of dense woods.


Hodge Podge went knock, knock, knock.

Then he sat back.

"Who is that?" said a man.

Hodge Podge sat still.

"Come in. Just push. Give it a shove," said the man.

Hodge Podge went in.


He had a glance at the room.

He was in a big kitchen.

The man in the kitchen had on a big hat.

"Well, well, what is this?" said the man.

"It's a hedgehog in the kitchen of the King of France."

"Just think of that!"

"Hello hedgehog. I am Vincent the cook of the King of France."

It is sad but true that hedgehogs can't talk.
Hodge Podge just looks up and grins.

Vince held up a jug and said,
"Have a glass of juice."
He held up some bread and said,
"Have some fresh bread."
Vince held up some fudge and said,
"Have some fudge too."

Hodge Podge was glad.  Hodge Podge nods his head.
Hodge Podge got a glass of juice and some fresh bread.
Hodge Podge got a lot of fudge.
But Hodge Podge had too much fudge.
When Hodge Podge was done, his tummy had a bulge.

Hodge Podge should have said thanks.
But then hedgehogs can't talk.
Hodge Podge gives another nod instead.
"Come back again soon," said Vince.
Hodge Podge left and went back to his hedge.

Hedgehogs can talk to other hedgehogs,
and Hodge Podge could tell his Mom
he met a man in a tall hat who gives hedgehogs
juice and bread and fudge.

# SECTION IV

## Teaching the Sounds

/ee/  /aw/  /ae/  /ie/  /oe/  /ue/

/ou/  /oi/  /er/  /ar/  /or/  /air/

# Parents/Teachers

This is the final section in the *Sound Steps to Reading* program. By now children are familiar with the structure of the lessons. They know the main spellings for all the consonants and for seven vowel sounds. At this point, children should be comfortable with the concept of spelling alternatives for one sound. All remaining lessons are on vowels, and all these vowels have spelling alternatives.

### Simple Vowels
Up to now, lessons have used 'simple' vowels, vowels with one clear sound. The sounds **/ee/** and **/aw/** are the last two simple vowels to teach. (Note: **/aw/** is a distinct vowel sound in some dialects, but a spelling alternative for **/o/** in others. Adjust your language and the lesson accordingly.)

### Diphthongs
Complex vowels, or 'diphthongs', are vowels that 'glide' between two sounds. For example, the sound **/oi/** is a glide between **/oh/** and **/ee/**. Diphthongs count as one vowel sound. There are six diphthongs in English. In four, the main spelling is split by a consonant: **/ae/** (*late*), **/ie/** (*fine*), **/oe/** (*bone*), **/ue/** (*cute*).

### Vowel + r
Nine vowels in English glide between a regular vowel and /r/ (back sides of the tongue against upper teeth). These are: **fir, far, for, fear, fair, fire, flour, cure, tour**. They are strongly affected by dialect. In some regions (UK, New England) the /r/ is dropped altogether, sounding '**eh**' or '**uh**' - "motherr" versus "mothuh."

Most vowel + r spellings are predictable and words with these spellings appear on the same pages as the main vowel sound. However, four vowel + r spellings need to be taught separately because of special issues.

### The Vowel Spelling Code

There are only five vowel letters, plus **y** and **r**, to represent 18 English vowel sounds. These letters are reused again and again for a variety of spelling alternatives. This single fact is the main cause of reading and spelling difficulties. If you keep the main issues clear, all child can manage this complexity with no difficulty. Please keep these important facts in mind:

**Digraphs and phonograms.** Most vowel sounds are written with letter pairs (digraphs) or with multi-letter sequences, called "phonograms" (h**igh**, b**ought**).

**Spelling alternatives.** There is more than one spelling for most vowel sounds.

**Sound alternatives.** Letters, digraphs, and phonograms – can stand for more than one sound (h**o**t/c**o**ld, f**i**n/f**i**nd, h**ea**t/h**ea**d, th**ough**/b**ough**). Parents and teachers must be aware what issue is the focus at any moment and help with appropriate language.   Children need to be secure about which letters work together to stand for one sound and which do not. **No guessing!**

## Visual Memory

To master spelling alternatives, children need to see many words.   Visual memory is the key.   And children must learn *which* spelling stands for *which* sound in *which* words. **This means lots of copying (saying each sound out loud), and spelling from dictation. Copying letters 'stamps' in the visual image, while saying the sounds as you write them, integrates visual, auditory, and motor cues, and dramatically speeds learning.**

To assist visual memory, words are segmented in the **Word Fun** exercises as before.  Children see how letters combine to stand for a single sound.  Words are grouped into sets to illustrate spelling patterns common to particular words.  This prevents common decoding errors like reading the word **'goat'** (3 sounds, 1 syllable) as **'go-at'** (4 sounds, 2 syllables).

During these final lessons many children will take off and start reading if they haven't done so already.   A child's brain is an amazing organ.   Children should move ahead as fast as they want to, providing they *do not skip any lessons*. Being a good reader at this level doesn't guarantee that they will be a good reader when words get longer and harder to read.   And it certainly does not guarantee they will be a good speller.   There are many helpful clues when you read, but no helpful clues when you write and spell.   Spelling patterns must be stored in memory so they can be retrieved effortlessly and automatically.

## Multi-syllable Words

Over the course of these lessons children have learned many multi-syllable words.   They are familiar with the suffixes '**ing**' and '**er,**' and names that end in **/ee/** spelled **y** (*Mooly*).   They know words that start with a weak '**uh**' sound (called a **schwa**), like '*across*' '*above*' and '*again.*'   They know simple compound words like '*Scotland*' and *hotdog*,' and complex compound words like '*English*,' '*instead*' and '*another.*'   They have read words like: '*kitchen*' '*happy*' '*chicken*' '*salad*' and '*hello.*'   Multi-syllable words are more common in the next lessons.   If a child thinks he *can't* read one of these words *do not supply the word.*   Say: "*You have seen words like this before.  Try and sound it out.*" If this is difficult, have him decode by syllable 'chunks.' **Model this process:**

> Start by isolating the first syllable: '*for*' in '**forget**'
> Segment these sounds: **/f/ /or/**   then blend back into the syllable: '*for*'
> Segment the next syllable: **/g/ /e/ /t/**. Blend to '*get*'.
> Now put the two syllables together and say: '**forget.**'

## the sound /ee/          A Mean Green Dragon

Read the story for enjoyment.  Do the listening exercise.  Reread the story and play the listening game.  Make the sound **/ee/** with a bright smile.  Go to Word Fun.

Dragons aren't real.
This story's not true.
But maybe, just maybe—
well, I'll leave it to you.

Charlie Cheetah woke from a dream.
He saw this thing in a stream.
He told his friends, "I crept up to see.
It had forty green teeth,
too many for me."

Zeke the Zebra saw it eat a hyena.
He said it was green from its head to its feet.
It looked terribly mean.
Not anything you'd want to meet.

### Listening for the sound /ee/

**Read each sentence below to the child.**

The sound you hear the most in this story is **/ee/**.  Watch my mouth when I say this sound.  **/ee/** [jaw up, bright smile]

Now you say the sound **/ee/**.  Say the word '**eat**' and listen for the sound /**ee**/.  It is the first sound.

Listen to these words and raise your hand when you hear the sound /**ee**/.  Tell me if it is the first, the middle, or the last sound.

| | | |
|---|---|---|
| **three** | **eagle** | **mean** |
| **street** | **see** | **green** |
| **scream** | **sneak** | **tea** |

I'm going to say the next word slowly.  Raise your hand when you hear the sound /**ee**/.

**z---e---b---r---a**          Push the sounds together to make the word.

If a child needs extra practice, do more words with /**ee**/.  Reread the story and play the listening game.  Then go ahead to Word Fun.

## the sound /ee/  Word Fun

Four spellings for the sound **/ee/** are taught in these lessons. One is familiar from words like '**be**' and '**he**'. **Do the copying and spelling exercises separately for each of these spellings. They are critical at this stage.**

# ee

| | | | |
|---|---|---|---|
| b---ee | bee | b---ee---f | beef |
| t---r---ee | tree | kn---ee | knee |
| f---ee---t | feet | h---ee---l | heel |
| ch---ee---k | cheek | g---ee---se | geese |
| qu---ee---n | queen | t---ee---th | teeth |
| sh---ee---p | sheep | wh---ee---l | wheel |
| | | | |
| d---ee---p | deep | f---ee---l | feel |
| f---ee---d | feed | m---ee---t | meet |
| n---ee---d | need | p---ee---k | peek |
| s---ee---m | seem | s---ee---n | seen |
| w---ee---k | week | w---ee---p | weep |
| c---r---ee---k | creek | g---r---ee---n | green |
| g---r---ee---t | greet | s---l---ee---p | sleep |
| s---l---ee---ve | sleeve | s---p---ee---d | speed |
| s---t---ee---p | steep | th---r---ee | three |

# the sound /ee/

## Words ending in the sound /z/ spelled <u>ze</u> or <u>se</u>

b---r---ee---ze    breeze       ch---ee---se       cheese

f---r---ee---ze    freeze       s---n---ee---ze       sneeze

s---qu---ee---ze   squeeze     wh---ee---ze        wheeze

## Words with the vowel sound /ee-er/ (counts as one vowel)

ch---eer       cheer       d---eer       deer

s---t---eer     steer       qu---eer      queer

# the sound /ee/

This is another common spelling for **/ee/**. SAY: *"We've seen this before for the sound **/e/** (head). This spelling is used for two sounds. Mostly, it's used for the sound **/ee/**."* **Do the copying and spelling exercises for this spelling.**

# ea

| | | | |
|---|---|---|---|
| ea---t | **eat** | p---ea | **pea** |
| s---ea | **sea** | b---ea---k | **beak** |
| m---ea---t | **meat** | r---ea---d | **read** |
| b---ea---ch | **beach** | p---ea---ch | **peach** |
| ea---ch | **each** | ea---s---t | **east** |
| h---ea---t | **heat** | l---ea---d | **lead** |
| l---ea--k | **leak** | l---ea---p | **leap** |
| m---ea---l | **meal** | n---ea---t | **neat** |
| r---ea---l | **real** | s---ea---t | **seat** |
| t---ea---m | **team** | w---ea--k | **weak** |
| ch---ea--p | **cheap** | ch---ea---t | **cheat** |
| l---ea---sh | **leash** | l---ea---ve | **leave** |
| r---ea---ch | **reach** | t---ea---ch | **teach** |

# ea

| | | | |
|---|---|---|---|
| b---ea---s---t | **beast** | c---r---ea---m | **cream** |
| l---ea---s---t | **least** | s---p--ea---k | **speak** |
| s---qu---ea---l | **squeal** | s---t---ea---l | **steal** |
| s---t---ea---m | **steam** | t---r---ea---t | **treat** |
| s---c---r---ea---m | **scream** | | |

## Words ending in the sound /z/ spelled <u>se</u>

| | | | |
|---|---|---|---|
| p---l---ea---se | **please** | t---ea---se | **tease** |

## Words ending in the sound /s/ spelled <u>se</u> and <u>ce</u>

| | | | |
|---|---|---|---|
| c---ea---se | **cease** | g---r---ea---se | **grease** |
| p---ea---ce | **peace** | | |

## Words with the vowel sound /ee-er/ spelled <u>ear</u>

| | | | |
|---|---|---|---|
| ear | **ear** | d---ear | **dear** |
| f---ear | **fear** | h---ear | **hear** |
| n---ear | **near** | r---ear | **rear** |
| sh---ear | **shear** | t---ear | **tear** |
| c---l---ear | **clear** | s---p---ear | **spear** |

---

Reminder: <u>**ea**</u> also stands for the sound /e/   <u>**head**</u>  <u>**bread**</u>

# the sound /ee/

The final **/ee/** in multi-syllable words is mainly spelled **y** and sometimes **ey**. We have seen this before in people's names. This is the first time the letter **y** has been featured. Children must practice copying and writing this letter.

# y        ey

Remember these names?

| Poppy | Vicky | Penny | Cathy | Mooly |
|-------|-------|-------|-------|-------|

| | | | | |
|-------|-------|-------|-------|-------|
| j---e---ll---y | jelly | t---u---mm---y | tummy |
| b---u---nn---y | bunny | s---u---nn---y | sunny |
| p---u---pp---y | puppy | k---i---tt---y | kitty |
| m---o---n---ey | money | v---a---ll---ey | valley |

| | | |
|-------|-------|-------|
| lucky | happy | silly |
| funny | jolly | runny |
| mummy | daddy | gloomy |
| nasty | messy | rusty |
| smelly | sleepy | ugly |
| key | donkey | honey |

**Special words:**       any       very
  Say: These words are    enny      vairy

146

# the sound /ee/

SAY: *"When this letter begins a word (point) it stands for a tiny /ee/ sound that you can hardly hear."* **Do the copying and spelling exercises.**

## y

ee---e---ll     yell        ee---e---s     yes

ee---e---t     yet         ee---ear     year

## e

SAY: Remember these words?

be      he      me      she      we

Try this:     z---e---b---r---a     zebra

**Special words:**     **here**       **these**
   Say, these words are    heer        theez

# Really Reading
## Reading words with the sound /ee/

Insist that children try to decode the 'big' words on their own: **began**, **after**, **reading**, **asleep**, **sudden**, **under**, **matter**. Help with '**Oh**' and '**don't**'.

## *Queen Jean's Big Feet*

Queen Jean had big feet.
She said, "Oh dear, I fear,
these feet can not be seen."
She began to weep.
A tear fell on her cheek.

Queen Jean hid her feet
in the sand at the sea.
She hid her feet in a stream.
She hid her feet in grass that was green.
She sat in deep weeds for a week.

No one can cheer up Queen Jean.
She will not be seen,
year after year after year.

One day, Queen Jean
was reading under a tree.
She fell asleep and a sudden breeze
blew her dress off her feet.

Then, Prince Preen
saw Queen Jean asleep under the tree.
It was easy to see Queen Jean's big feet.
Prince Preen began to speak:

He said, "I love you Queen Jean.
Your feet don't matter to me."

# Really Reading
### Reading words that end in the sound /ee/ spelled y

## *Runny Jelly*

Mom put jelly on a bun.
The jelly sat in the sun.
It was sunny.
The jelly got runny.

Betty fed it to kitty.
Such a pity.
The kitty got messy.
The kitty got sticky.

Betty fed it to Billy.
Such a pity.
Billy got messy.
Billy got sticky.

Betty was jolly.
Betty was funny.
But Betty was silly,
but Betty was bad.

*NOTE: Many children will be able to start reading the parent stories by now. If a child had no difficulty reading the two stories above, let him/her try to read the parent story for the sound /ee/: "The Mean Green Dragon."*

# the sound /aw/   Austin Auk Goes for a Walk

Read the story for enjoyment.  Do the listening exercise.  Read the story again and play the listening game.  Depending on your  dialect, say:  1) "This is another story for the sound /o/" (**hot**)  OR  2) "The sound you heard the most was /**aw**/."

Austin Auk often swam in the sea or stood on the shore.
One day he thought, "I'll go for a walk."
He popped out of the water and wandered off.

Austin went on his jaunt just after dawn.
He waddled up the beach and out across a lawn.
His mom never knew he was gone.

The sight of Austin caused a hawk
to stop in mid-air and let out a squawk.
He started to fall and grabbed onto a branch with his claws

---

## Listening for the Sound /aw/

***Do this lesson only if there is a separate /aw/ sound in your dialect.***

**Read each sentence below to the child.**

The sound you hear the most in this story is /**aw**/.  Watch my mouth when I say this sound.  /**aw**/ [jaw down, lips rounded and forward.]

Now you say the sound /**aw**/.   Say the word '**auk**' and listen for the sound /**aw**/.  Is it the first sound or the last sound?

Listen to these words and raise your hand when you hear the sound /**aw**/.  Then tell me if it is the first, the middle, or the last sound.

| | | | | | |
|---|---|---|---|---|---|
| **hawk** | **law** | **small** | **fawn** | **talk** | **paw** |
| **awful** | **pause** | **jaunt** | | | |

I'm going to say the next word slowly.  Raise your hand when you hear the sound /**aw**/.

**d---augh---t---er**

Push the sounds together to make the word.

If your child needs extra practice, do more words with /aw/.  Reread the story and do this listening game.  Then move ahead to Word Fun.

## the sound /aw/ or /o/     Word Fun

There are five spellings for the sound **/aw/** or **/o/** in this section: SAY *either:* "Here are some new ways to spell the sound **/o/** (*hot*) OR "The sound **/aw/** has many different spellings." **Do the copying and spelling exercises for each new spelling separately**.

# aw

| | | | |
|---|---|---|---|
| j---aw | jaw | p---aw | paw |
| c---l---aw | claw | f---aw---n | fawn |
| h---aw---k | hawk | d---r---aw | draw |
| | | | |
| l---aw | law | r---aw | raw |
| s---aw | saw | th---aw | thaw |
| d---aw---n | dawn | l---aw---n | lawn |
| sh---aw---l | shawl | s---t---r---aw | straw |
| | | | |
| c---r---aw---l | crawl | aw---f---u---l | awful |

# au

| | | | |
|---|---|---|---|
| au---k | auk | h---au---n---t | haunt |
| h---au---l | haul | f---au---l---t | fault |
| j---au---n---t | jaunt | v---au---l---t | vault |

Note: the sound **/z/** is spelled <u>se</u> in these words:

| | | | |
|---|---|---|---|
| c---au---se | cause | p---au---se | pause |

# the sound /aw/ or /o/

These spellings are known as **L-controlled and W-controlled spellings**, because they signal how the preceding/or following vowel is pronounced. SAY *either*: "Here is another way to spell the sound **/o/** or "Here is another way to spell the sound **/aw/**." Point to patterns where **a** stands for the sound **/aw/** before **/l/** and after **/w/**. **Do the copying and writing exercises**.

## a (l)

| | | | |
|---|---|---|---|
| b---a---ll | ball | f---a---ll | fall |
| b---a---l---d | bald | p---a---l---m | palm |
| a---ll | all | c---a---ll | call |
| h---a---ll | hall | t---a---ll | tall |
| c---a---l---m | calm | f---a---l---se | false |
| h---a---l---t | halt | s---m---a---ll | small |

## (w) a

| | | | |
|---|---|---|---|
| s---w---a---n | swan | w---a---s---p | wasp |
| w---a---t---er | water | w---a---tch | watch |
| s---w---a---p | swap | s---w---a---t | swat |
| w---a---ll | wall | w---a---n---d | wand |
| w---a---n---t | want | w---a---sh | wash |
| w---a---n---d---er | wander | | |

SAY: "In these word, four letters stand for only one sound."

| ough | | augh | |
|---|---|---|---|
| ough---t | ought | c--augh---t | caught |
| b---ough---t | bought | t---augh---t | taught |
| th---ough---t | thought | d---augh-t-er | daughter |

152

# Really Reading

## Reading words with the sound /aw/

Help the child read the words '**Austin**' '**fly**' '**daughter**'.

## *Austin Auk's Long Walk*

Austin Auk was small.
But he could swim.
He could fly.
He could walk.
He could catch a fish.
Austin Auk could do a lot of things.

Austin went on a walk.
He went on a path and on a lawn.
Austin saw a hawk, a swan, and a fawn.
The hawk and the swan did not think that
Austin could swim, and fly, and catch a fish.
They thought that Austin was odd.

But the hawk was wrong.
Austin could fly.
The swan was wrong.
Austin could swim and catch a fish.

Shaun and his daughter saw Austin on the lawn too.
Then Shaun read a book.
Shaun saw in his book that Austin was an auk.
He read that auks live in the water.
Shaun and his daughter will help Austin get back to the water.
They will help him get back to his mom.

**Children can also try to read parent version of Austin Auk.**

# the sound /ae/   Jicky-Jo-Jay Saves Abe the Ape

Read this story for enjoyment.  Do the listening exercise.  Reread the story and play the listening game.  Explain that a 'glade' is a shady grassy spot.

Up on the hill in Zay-O-Zay
the grass in the glade
where the apes always play
was in shade.

It was late in the day
and some men laid in wait.
"We'll get one today."
"Put out the bait."

On the grass in the glade
where the apes always play
sat Abe, baby Abe.
He was three and a day.

---

## Listening for the sound /ae/

**Read each sentence below to the child.**

The sound you hear the most in this story is /**ae**/

Watch my mouth when I say this sound.  /**ae**/ [Jaw down for /**e**/ -- glide to /**ee**/ by closing your jaw.]

Now you say the sound /**ae**/.  Say the word '**ate**'.  The sound /**ae**/ is the first sound, isn't it?  Now say the word '**gate**'.  Is the sound /**ae**/ at the beginning or in the middle?

Listen to these words and raise your hand when you hear the sound /**ae**/.  Tell me if it is the first, the middle, or the last sound.

| | | | | |
|---|---|---|---|---|
| **day** | **ape** | **plate** | **play** | **able** |
| **great** | **skate** | **stay** | **brave** | |

I'm going to say the next word slowly.  Raise you hand when you hear the sound /**ae**/.

    **t---a---b---u---l**

Now push the sounds together to make the word.

If the child needs extra practice, do more words with 'ae'.  Reread the story and play the listening game.  Move to Word Fun.

## the sound /ae/     Word Fun

There are four spellings for the sound **/ae/** in this section. Write the spelling **a-e** on a piece of paper or on the board. SAY: "The letters in this spelling are **always split apart**, but they still work together. The *sound* **/ae/** happens at here [point to the letter **a**.]"

[Teacher's note. To complicate matters, the final **e** often plays two roles. It works with the preceding vowel *and* with the consonant in words ending **ge** **ve** **ce** **se**].

**Do the copying and spelling exercises for each new spelling separately.**

# a-e

| | | | |
|---|---|---|---|
| a---p-e | **ape** | c---a---g-e | **cage** |
| c---a---k-e | **cake** | c---a---v-e | **cave** |
| g---a---t-e | **gate** | l---a---k-e | **lake** |
| m---a---n-e | **mane** | w---a---v-e | **wave** |
| a---ge | **age** | a---t-e | **ate** |
| b---a---k-e | **bake** | c---a---m-e | **came** |
| d---a---t-e | **date** | g---a---m-e | **game** |
| g---a---v-e | **gave** | h---a---t-e | **hate** |
| l---a---n-e | **lane** | l---a---t-e | **late** |
| m---a---d-e | **made** | m---a---k-e | **make** |
| n---a---m-e | **name** | p---a---l-e | **pale** |
| p---a---v-e | **pave** | r---a---t-e | **rate** |
| r---a---v-e | **rave** | s---a---l-e | **sale** |
| s---a---v-e | **save** | t---a---k-e | **take** |
| t---a---l-e | **tale** | t---a---m-e | **tame** |
| w---a---d-e | **wade** | w---a---k-e | **wake** |

# the sound /ae/

# a-e

| | | | |
|---|---|---|---|
| wh---a---l-e | whale | b---l---a---z-e | blaze |
| g---r---a---p-e | grape | p---l---a---n-e | plane |

| | | | |
|---|---|---|---|
| sh---a---d-e | shade | sh---a---k-e | shake |
| sh---a---p-e | shape | sh---a---v-e | shave |
| a---w---a--k-e | awake | b---r---a--k-e | brake |
| b---r---a---v-e | brave | f---l---a--m-e | flame |
| g---r---a---d-e | grade | g---r---a---z-e | graze |
| p---l---a---t-e | plate | s--c---a--l-e | scale |
| s---k--a---t-e | skate | s--t---a--g-e | stage |
| t---r---a---d-e | trade | | |

## Words ending in the sound /s/ spelled <u>ce</u> or <u>se</u>

The letter <u>**e**</u> plays two roles – working with the preceding vowel and with the letter <u>**c**</u>.

| | | | |
|---|---|---|---|
| f---a---c-e | face | r---a---c-e | race |
| ch---a---s-e | chase | g---r---a---c-e | grace |
| p---l---a---c-e | place | s---p---a---c-e | space |

# the sound /ae/

# ai

| | | | |
|---|---|---|---|
| n---ai---l | nail | p---ai---l | pail |
| r---ai---n | rain | s---ai---l | sail |
| t---ai---l | tail | ch---ai---n | chain |
| s---n---ai---l | snail | t---r---ai---n | train |

| | | | |
|---|---|---|---|
| ai---m | aim | f---ai---l | fail |
| g---ai---n | gain | m---ai---l | mail |
| p---ai---d | paid | p---ai---n | pain |
| w---ai---t | wait | c---l---ai---m | claim |
| b---r---ai---d | braid | b---r---ai---n | brain |
| d---r---ai---n | drain | g---r---ai---n | grain |
| p---l---ai---n | plain | S---p---ai---n | Spain |
| s---t---ai---n | stain | t---r---ai---l | trail |

| | |
|---|---|
| a---f---r---ai---d | afraid |
| e---x---p---l---ai---n | explain |

# the sound /ae/

# ay

| | | | |
|---|---|---|---|
| h---ay | hay | j---ay | jay |
| p---l---ay | play | t---r---ay | tray |

| | | | |
|---|---|---|---|
| a---w---ay | away | c---l---ay | clay |
| d---ay | day | g---ay | gay |
| g--r---ay | gray | l---ay | lay |
| m---ay | may | p---ay | pay |
| p--r---ay | pray | s---ay | say |
| s---t---ay | stay | w---ay | way |

## Long Words

| | |
|---|---|
| a---l---w---ay---s | always |
| c---r---ay---o---n | crayon |
| m---ay---b---e | maybe |
| t---o---d---ay | today |

# the sound /ae/

The letter **a** appears again in another role - - representing the sound **/ae/** in the accented syllable of a multi-syllable word.   Don't try to explain this to the child just yet!

# a

| | | | |
|---|---|---|---|
| b---a---b---y | baby | b---a---c---o---n | bacon |
| c---r---a---z---y | crazy | g---r---a---v---y | gravy |
| l---a---d---y | lady | l---a---z---y | lazy |
| n---a---v---y | navy | sh---a---d---y | shady |
| t---a---s---t-e | taste | ch---a---n---g-e | change |

## Tricky words

The faint letter **u** stands for a tiny **/uh/** sound.  (*It is not 'silent'*)

| | | | |
|---|---|---|---|
| a---b---ᴜ---l | able | c---r---a---d---ᴜ---l | cradle |
| f---a---b---ᴜ---l | fable | t---a---b---ᴜ---l | table |
| s---t---a---b---ᴜ---l | stable | d---a---n---g---er | danger |

## Special Words

| | | | |
|---|---|---|---|
| eigh---t | eight | b---r---ea---k | break |
| g---r---ea---t | great | s---t----ea---k | steak |

---

**a**  also stands for the sounds **/a/** (cat, hat) and **/aw/** or **/o/** (ball, talk).

# Really Reading
### Reading words with the sound /ae/

Help read the words **Birthday, I.**

# Kate's Birthday

"Mommy, wake up, wake up!
It's after eight.  Mommy, it's late.
Make me some eggs and bacon.
Bake me a great big cake.
Make me a milk shake."

"Can Kay come today?
I want to play games with Kay.
Take us to see Jake.
We can race to the edge of the lake."

"Mom, let's take Kay and Jake
on a big tall ship with a sail.
We can sail away on the sea.
We can see lots of fish.
We can see a big whale."

"Take us on a train or a plane
way away up, off into space,

all the way to France and Spain.
It will be great."

Mom said, "Wait!
Kate, this is crazy.
This does not make sense.
Stop this, I say.
We can't do all this in a day."

But Kate did not stop.
Kate will not wait.
Kate ran away.
Kate has not been seen to this day.

[Some children may be able to read the parent story: **Jicky-Jo-Jay Saves Abe the Ape.**]

## the sound /ie/          Nigel the Nice

Read this story for enjoyment.  Do the listening exercise.  Reread the story and play the listening game.   Go on to Word Fun.

Nigel the Nice was a knight.
He was quite a sight
in an iron suit that was too bright.
Nigel was mild.  He was kind.  He was nice.
But Nigel takes flight when the other knights fight.

"Fie on you Nigel," said King Brian the Wise.
"You're idle and useless.  Get out of my sight.
Fly to the wild and find Sir Guy.
If we don't find him soon, he might die.

---

### Listening for the sound /ie/

Read each sentence to your child

The sound you hear the most in this story is /ie/.

Watch my mouth when I say this sound.  /ie/  [jaw down for /ah/ and glide up to /ee/]

Now you say the sound /ie/.

Say the word 'ice' and listen for the sound /ie/.  It's the first sound isn't it?

Listen to these words and raise your hand when you hear the sound /ie/.  Is it the first, middle or the last sound?

|        |        |       |
|--------|--------|-------|
| cry    | fight  | idle  |
| wild   | smile  | die   |

I'm going to say the next word slowly.  Raise your hand when you hear the sound /ie/.

t---i---g---er          tiger

Push the sounds together to make the word.

---------------------------------------------------------------------------------------

If your child needs extra practice, do more words with /ie/.  Reread the story and play the listening game.  Then move ahead to Word Fun.

**the sound /ie/**       **Word Fun**

There are four spellings for the sound **/ie/** in these lessons.  SAY: *"In this spelling, the letters are usually split apart [point], just like we learned before."*  **Do the copying and spelling exercises for each new spelling separately.**

# ie

| die | lie | pie | tie |
|-----|-----|-----|-----|

# i-e

| b---i---ke | bike | d---i---ve | dive |
|------------|------|------------|------|
| h---i---ke | hike | k---i---te | kite |
| kn---i---f-e | knife | p---i---ne | pine |
| b---i---te | bite | ch---i---me | chime |
| d---i---ne | dine | f---i---ne | fine |
| f---i---ve | five | h---i---de | hide |
| l---i---fe | life | l---i---ke | like |
| l---i---ne | line | l---i---ve | live |
| m---i---le | mine | m---i---ne | mine |
| n---i---ne | nine | p---i--le | pile |
| qu---i---te | quite | r--i---de | ride |
| r---i---pe | ripe | sh---i---ne | shine |
| s---i---de | side | t--i---me | time |
| v---i---ne | vine | | |

# the sound /ie/

# i-e

| | | | |
|---|---|---|---|
| a---l---i---ve | **alive** | a---rr---i---ve | **arrive** |
| d---r---i---ve | **drive** | p---r---i---ze | **prize** |
| s---l---i---de | **slide** | s---m---i---le | **smile** |
| s---t---r---i---pe | **stripe** | | |

## Words ending in the sound /s/ spelled <u>ce</u>

| | | | |
|---|---|---|---|
| i---ce | ice | m---i---ce | mice |
| n---i---ce | nice | r---i---ce | rice |
| p---r---i---ce | price | s---l---i---ce | slice |

## Words with the vowel sound 'ie-er'   *('ire' counts as one vowel sound)*

| | | | |
|---|---|---|---|
| f---ire | fire | h---ire | hire |
| t---ire | tire | w---ire | wire |
| s---p---ire | spire | | |

# the sound /ie/

# i

| | | | |
|---|---|---|---|
| b---l---i---n---d | blind | ch---i---l---d | child |
| f---i---n---d | find | k---i---n---d | kind |
| m---i---l---d | mild | m---i---n---d | mind |
| p---i---n---t | pint | w---i---l---d | wild |

## Long Words

Show children how to split the syllables with adjacent vowel sounds (see words on the rignt).

| | | | |
|---|---|---|---|
| b---e---h---i---n---d | behind | l---i--/--o---n | lion |
| p---i---l---o---t | pilot | qu---i--/--e---t | quiet |
| t---i---g---er | tiger | | |

**Special words:**   iron      liar (li/ar)

---

Remember: **i** also stands for the sound /i/   **hit** **trip**

# the sound /ie/

SAY: "When **/ie/** is the last sound in a word, this is the main way to spell it."

# y

| | | | |
|---|---|---|---|
| c---r---y | **cry** | f---l---y | **fly** |
| s---k---y | **sky** | t---r---y | **try** |

| | | | |
|---|---|---|---|
| b---y | **by** | d---r---y | **dry** |
| f---r---y | **fry** | m---y | **my** |
| p---l---y | **ply** | p---r---y | **pry** |
| sh---y | **shy** | s---p---y | **spy** |
| s---l---y | **sly** | s---t---y | **sty** |
| wh---y | **why** | | |

**Special words:**   eye   buy   goodbye

Define:   **by**   **bye**   **buy**
  beside   goodbye   purchase

---

Remember: **y** also stands for the sound **/ee/** in **baby** **bunny**

# the sound /ie/

Here the sound **/ie/** is spelled with three letters.  Remind the child that this has happened before with the spellings:  **<u>dge</u>**  and  **<u>tch</u>**.

# igh

| | | | |
|---|---|---|---|
| f---igh---t | **fight** | kn---igh---t | knight |
| l---igh---t | **light** | th---igh | thigh |
| | | | |
| h---igh | **high** | m---igh---t | **might** |
| n---igh-t | **night** | r---igh---t | **right** |
| s---igh---t | **sight** | t---igh---t | **tight** |
| b---r---igh---t | **bright** | f---l---igh---t | **flight** |
| f---r---igh---t | **fright** | p---l---igh---t | **plight** |

## Really Reading

### Reading words with the sound /ie/
Insist that the child tries to read the words **little, animal**. Help with **don't**.

## *Why Lee Lion Does Not Like a Lion's Life*

Once upon a time there was a little lion.
His name was Lee.
Lee was sad and gloomy.
He was quiet and shy.
His mom and dad did not know why.

Lee Lion kept his thoughts to himself.
He kept his thoughts in his head.
This is what his thoughts said:

"Lions stay awake all night,
and sleep in the bright sunlight.
Lions have to snooze all day
while the other animals run and play."

"The other animals smile.
The other animals have a nice life.
I can't have any fun
if I sleep all day in the sun."

"I can't hike up a hill and fly a kite
I can't ride a bike.  I can't slide on a slide
I can't play 'I Spy' or hide and seek,
if I am always asleep."

"I don't look good
like an animal should.
I'm tan from my head to my tail
I don't have any spots.
I don't have any stripes."

"Why can't I be a tiger?
Or maybe a zebra?
I would look fine,
if I was bright white
with nice black stripes."

"I feel just awful.
I hate my life."
Lee Lion began to sigh.
Lee Lion began to cry.
His dad said, "My, my."

"What's all this?  What is wrong?
Wait until you get big and strong.
One day, some time soon,
Lee Lion will be king of the beasts.
Life will be one big feast.
Things will be alright."

Lee Lion gave his dad a big bright smile,
But he didn't think he was right.

[Note:  Some children may be able to read the parent story:  **Nigel the Nice]**

# the sound /oe/   Mole's Home Biznis

Read the story for enjoyment and do the listening exercise.  The sound **/oe/** is made by gliding between the sound **/u/** and **/oo/**.

Mole poked his nose out of his hole
He reached for his Daily Globe
that was stuck in the snow.
"Well, well.  It's cold, it's cold.
I'd better go down below."

As mole went into his underground burrow
his face had a frown, his forehead a furrow.
He was, as usual, alone at home.
Mole mumbled, "Home alone. Home alone."

Mole had a habit of saying things over,
and over and over.

---

## Listening for the sound /oe/

### Read each sentence to your child.

The sound you hear the most in this story is /**oe**/.

Watch my mouth when I say this sound.  /**oe**/. [start with an '**uh**' and glide to '**oo**']

Now you say the sound /**oe**/.   Say the word '**old**' and listen for the sound /**oe**/.  It's the first sound isn't it?

Listen to these words and raise your hand when you hear the sound /**oe**/.  Tell me is it is the first, the middle, or the last sound.

| | | |
|---|---|---|
| **mole** | **open** | **slow** |
| **own** | **home** | **go** |
| **know** | **float** | **yellow** |

I'm going to say the next word slowly.  Raise your hand when you hear the sound /**oe**/.

**c---o---c---oa**

Push the sounds together to make the word.

If the child needs extra practice, do more words with **/oe/**.  Reread the story and do the listening game.  Then move ahead to Word Fun.

## the sound /oe/          Word Fun

There are four spellings for the sound **/oe/** in this section.  Point out that the main spelling for **/oe/** is usually split apart, just as before.  **Do the copying and spelling exercises for each page separately.**

# oe

doe          goes          hoe          toe

# o-e

b---o---n-e          bone          c---o---n-e          cone

h---o---l-e          hole          m---o---l-e          mole

r---o---b-e          robe          r---o---p-e          rope

c--o---d-e          code          ch---o--k-e          choke

h---o---m-e          home          h---o---p-e          hope

j--o--k-e          joke          r---o---d-e          rode

n--o---t-e          note          qu--o---t-e          quote

v--o---t-e          vote          wh---o---l-e          whole

wr---o---t-e          wrote          z---o---n-e          zone

a---l---o---n-e          alone          g---l---o---b-e          globe

g--r--o---v-e          grove          s--l---o--p-e          slope

s---m---o--k-e          smoke          s---p---o--k-e          spoke

th--r---o---n-e          throne          a---l---o---n---e          alone

**Special word:**          **ph---o---n-e**          **phone**
                    SAY:                    'fone'

170

# o-e

words ending with the sound /z/ spelled z or s

| | | | |
|---|---|---|---|
| ch---o---se | chose | c---l---o---se | close |
| d---o---ze | doze | f---r---o---ze | froze |
| h---o---se | hose | n---o---se | nose |
| p---o---se | pose | r---o---se | rose |
| th---o---se | those | | |

---

# o

| | go | | no | | so |
|---|---|---|---|---|---|
| c---o---l---t | colt | f---o---l---d | fold | | |
| g---o---l---d | gold | p---o---s---t | post | | |
| b---o---th | both | c---o---l---d | cold | | |
| c---o---z---y | cozy | d---o---n'—t | don't | | |
| h---e---ll---o | hello | h---o---l---d | hold | | |
| m---o---s---t | most | o---l---d | old | | |
| o---n---l---y | only | r---o---ll | roll | | |
| r---o---s---y | rosy | s---o---l---d | sold | | |
| t---o---l---d | told | w---o---n'—t | won't | | |
| a---l---s—o | also | a---l---m---o---s---t | almost | | |

Remember: **o** also stands for the sound **/o/**. **hot**   **dog**

# the sound /oe/

# oa

| | | | |
|---|---|---|---|
| b---oa---t | **boat** | c---oa---ch | **coach** |
| c---oa---t | **coat** | f---oa---l | **foal** |
| g---oa---t | **goat** | t---oa---d | **toad** |

| | | | |
|---|---|---|---|
| f---oa---m | **foam** | g---oa---l | **goal** |
| l---oa---f | **loaf** | l---oa---n | **loan** |
| r---oa---d | **road** | r---oa---m | **roam** |
| s---oa---k | **soak** | s---oa---p | **soap** |
| b---oa---s---t | **boast** | c---oa---s---t | **coast** |
| f---l---oa---t | **float** | r---oa---s---t | **roast** |
| th---r---oa---t | **throat** | t---oa---s---t | **toast** |

the sound /oe/

# OW

| | | | |
|---|---|---|---|
| m---ow | mow | r---ow | row |
| b---ow---l | bowl | c---r---ow | crow |
| | | | |
| l---ow | low | t---ow | tow |
| kn---ow | know | ow---n | own |
| sh---ow | show | b---l---ow | blow |
| g---r---ow | grow | s---l---ow | slow |
| s--n---ow | snow | th---r---ow | throw |
| | | | |
| e---l---b---ow | elbow | f---e---ll---ow | fellow |
| p---i---ll---ow | pillow | y---e---ll---ow | yellow |

# Really Reading
## Reading words with the sound /oe/

Insist that the child *tries* to read words: **rodent, animal, beaver, badger**. Help with unfamiliar spellings like **are, gnaw, mouse, gopher, squirrel**. This is the first piece of non-fiction. Tell children reading is not only fun, but a way to learn about something interesting.

## *What is a Rodent?*

A rodent is the name of a group of animals. A group must be alike in some way.

All rodents have two big front teeth that grow and grow. A rodent is an animal that gnaws its food. Gnaw means to bite with the front teeth. Gnaw means to bite over and over. Rodents can chew plants and nuts.

All rodents gnaw. They all have two big front teeth. They eat plants. These animals are rodents.

> mouse
> rat
> vole
> gopher
> beaver
> squirrel

Some rodents are big and some are small. Some live in trees. Some live in holes. Some live in the grass and in woods.

You may not know all these animals.

A vole is small like a mouse. It has a bigger body. It does not have a long tail like mice and rats.

A beaver is big. It can make a dam in a stream with mud and twigs. A beaver has very strong teeth. It can gnaw a tree and knock it over. A beaver can swim and walk on land.

A squirrel lives in a tree. It eats nuts. It can find nuts in trees and on the grass. It can gnaw the shell off the nut. It hides nuts in holes in trees. Then it will have food when it is too cold to find nuts.

A gopher lives in a hole. A gopher gnaws the roots of plants from its hole. When it eats the roots, it kills the plant.

The names 'mole' and 'badger' are not on the list of rodents.

A mole is not a rodent. Moles do not gnaw. They do not eat plants. Moles eat insects. Moles live in a hole. Moles make little hills when they dig out the hole. Moles are almost blind. They stay close to home.

A badger is not a rodent. A badger lives in a hole like a mole.

But a badger is not like a mole. A badger goes hunting. It eats meat and not insects. Badgers catch mice and rats. Badgers are not almost blind like a mole. Badgers have good eyesight. Badgers are clever. They spy on other animals. They can steal meat from big animals like panthers.

[Note: Some children may want to read the parent story: **Mole's Home Biznis.** Be sure to point out Mole's misspelling of 'biznis'.]

# the sound /ue/  O. U. Mule's Report

Read the story and then do the listening exercise.  Read the story again and play the listening game.  *This sound is not easy to hear*, and some people can't tell the difference between **/ue/** and **/oo/**.  Children should watch your mouth as you say a smiling, audible **/ee/** gliding to an **/oo/**.  Tell the child that a mule is like a horse and works on a farm.

O.U. Mule worked on his report.
On Tuesday at ten, it was due.
Mule had a meeting with Hugh.
It was Hugh's job to insure
that the mules were happy and secure.

At ten o-clock right on cue,
Mule said: "We are not happy mules.
Remember, mules are stubborn and can refuse
to pull ploughs, or carts, or tools."

---

## Listening for the sound /ue/

**Read each sentence below the child.**

The sound you hear the most in this story is /**ue**/.

Watch my mouth when I say this sound.  /**ue**/ [Begin with smiling **/ee/** gliding to **/oo/**].

Now you say the sound /**ue**/.   Say the word '**cute**' and listen for the sound /**ue**/.  Is it the first, the middle, or the last sound?

Listen to these words and raise your hand when you hear the sound /**ue**/.  Tell me if it is the first sound, the last sound, or in the middle.

| | | |
|---|---|---|
| **use** | **mule** | **few** |
| **music** | **refuse** | **cue** |

I'm going to say the next word slowly.  Raise your hand when you hear the sound /**ue**/.

**h---u---m---a---n**

Push the sounds together and say this word.

---

## the sound /ue/      Word Fun

There are three spellings for the sound **/ue/** in this section. This is not a common sound. Use your discretion with these words. Some words may too hard for some children at this stage. **Do the copying and writing exercises.**

# u-e

| | | | |
|---|---|---|---|
| c---u---be | cube | m---u---le | mule |
| c---ue | cue | c---u---te | cute |
| h---u---ge | huge | f---u---me---s | fumes |

**words ending in the sound 'z' spelled <u>se</u>**

| | | | |
|---|---|---|---|
| u---se | use | f---u---se | fuse |
| a---cc---u---se | accuse | a---m---u---se | amuse |
| e---x---c---u---se | excuse | r---e---f---u---se | refuse |

**Words with vowel sound 'ue-er'**

| | | | |
|---|---|---|---|
| c---ure | cure | f---ur---y | fury |
| p---ure | pure | s---e---c---ure | secure |

# U

| | | | |
|---|---|---|---|
| b---u---g---u---l | bugle | c---u---p---i---d | cupid |
| h---u---m---a---n | human | m---u---s---i---c | music |
| p---u---p---i---l | pupil | | |

-------------------------------------------------------------------

<u>u</u> also stands for the sound /u/ like **cut** **duck**

# Really Reading
## Reading words with the sound /ue/

Help with the hard words, and new words 'Hugh' 'for'.  Watch out.  Children can only read and understand this after they have heard the whole story from the Storybook.


O.U. Mule told Hugh that the mules
did not like a few things.
It was Hugh's job to help the mules.

The mules did not have a clean stable.
The stable was not fresh and pure.

The mules had no heating and lighting.
They got cold.  They could not read any books.

O.U. Mule told Hugh the mules had no music.
He said that mules liked tunes and duets.

Do you think that O.U. Mule asked Hugh for too much?

Do you think that mules really need heating and lighting?
Do you think that mules can read?
Do you think that mules need a good view?
Do you think that mules need music in the stable?



From this point forward, children should try to read the Parent version of the story as well.   Most children will be able to read nearly all the Parent stories with very little help.

## the sound /ou/          Olly Owl Gets Out

Read the story for enjoyment.  Do the listening exercise.  Reread the story and play the listening game.  Go to Word Fun.

The sun was down past the house on the hill.
The shops in the town, all still.
Not a sound on the hill.
Not a sound.

In the grove below,
where the beech and the oak
and the willows grow,
there was a crowd on the ground and all around.
It was loud.  Oh so loud!

The sing-a-long was going strong,
with everyone singing a different song.

---

**Listening for the sound /ou/**

**Read each sentence to your child.**

The sound you hear the most in this story is /**ou**/.

Watch my mouth when I say this sound.  /**ou**/  [Glide from /**a**/ to /**oo/**]

Now you say the sound /**ou**/.  Say the word '**house**' and listen for the sound /**ou**/.  Is it the first, the middle or the last sound?

Listen to these words and raise your hand when you hear the sound /**ou**/.  Tell me if it is the first, the middle, or the last sound.

| | | |
|---|---|---|
| **out** | **mouth** | **how** |
| **shout** | **owl** | **frown** |
| **cow** | **ouch** | **ground** |

I'm going to say the next word slowly.  Raise your hand when you hear the sound /**ou**/.

   **a---r---ou---n---d**

Push the sounds together to make the word.

-------------------------------------------------------------------------------------
If your child needs extra practice, do more words with /**ou**/.  Reread the story and play the listening game.  Then move ahead to Word Fun.

## the sound /ou/     Word Fun

Parents/Teachers. There are only two spellings for the sound **/ou/**.
**Do the copying and writing exercises.**

# OU

| | | | |
|---|---|---|---|
| m---ou---th | mouth | c---l---ou---d | cloud |
| h---ou--n---d | hound | t---r---ou---t | trout |

| | | | |
|---|---|---|---|
| ou---ch | ouch | ou---t | out |
| sh---ou---t | shout | s---ou---th | south |
| a--b---ou---t | about | g---r---ou--n---d | ground |
| c---ou--n---t | count | f---ou--n---d | found |
| p---ou--n---d | pound | p---r---ou---d | proud |
| r---ou--n---d | round | s---ou--n---d | sound |
| a--r---ou--n---d | around | | |

Words ending in the sound **/s/** spelled <u>ce</u> *or* <u>se</u>

| | | | |
|---|---|---|---|
| b---l---ou---se | blouse | b---ou--n---ce | bounce |
| h---ou---se | house | m---ou---se | mouse |
| ou--n---ce | ounce | p---ou--n---ce | pounce |

Words with the vowel sound '**ou-er**'

| | | | |
|---|---|---|---|
| our | our | f---l---our | flour |
| (h)our | hour | s---our | sour |

**h** is not sounded.

180

# the sound /ou/

## ow

| | | | |
|---|---|---|---|
| c—ow | cow | ow---l | owl |
| c---l---ow---n | clown | c---r---ow---n | crown |
| | | | |
| b---ow | bow | h—ow | how |
| n—ow | now | w---ow | wow |
| d---ow---n | down | h---ow---l | howl |
| t---ow---n | town | b---r---ow---n | brown |
| c---r---ow---d | crowd | d---r---ow---n | drown |
| f---r---ow---n | frown | g---r---ow---l | growl |
| p---r---ow---l | prowl | s---c---ow---l | scowl |

| | | | |
|---|---|---|---|
| f---l---ow---er | flower | sh---ow---er | shower |
| t---ow---el<br>This says 'towl' | towel | t---ow---er | tower |

---------------------------------------------------------------------------------------

Remember **<u>ow</u>** also stands for the sound **/oe/** **<u>blow</u>** **<u>grow</u>**

## *Olly Owl*

Olly Owl thinks he is wise.
Olly Owl likes to tell other animals what to do.
Olly told Mole that he didn't know how to spell.
But Olly can't spell much better than Mole.

Olly did not like the cow singing 'how now brown cow.'
He did not like Hal Hound's howling.
He did not like Min Mouse and her baby squeaking and eeking.
He did not like them singing all at once.
Olly told them to stop.

Olly was rude.
He said the singing was foul.
He said the singing sounds sour.
He said the singing went on too long.
He said it went on for one hour.

That is a long time to listen to a cow, and a hound,
and a mouse, and a pig, and a flock of sheep singing at once.
I would not like it.  Would you?

Hal Hound asked Olly Owl to sing along too.
But he didn't ask in a nice way.
Hal Hound was not polite.
He said "sing along or be gone."

Min Mouse was not nice.
She told Olly Owl to sing along or get out.
The animals would not do what Olly Owl told them to do.
Olly didn't get his way.  Olly could not win.
So Olly flew off to the house on the hill.
There wasn't a sound on the hill.
Not a sound.

## the sound /oi/     How Roy Stopped Making Noise

Read the story for enjoyment. Do the listening exercise. The sound /oi/ is made by gliding between /aw/ and /ee/.

The Royal Family in the far-off land of Broy-Bimini
were rich!
They were spoiled.
They had one hundred chests of gold coins.

The king has a turquoise blue Rolls-Royce.
The Queen has one thousand paintings in oil.
And Prince Roy and Princess Joyce,
Well—
They have their choice of one million toys.

---

### Listening for the sound /oi/

**Read each sentence to your child.**

The sound you heard the most in this story was /**oi**/.

Watch my mouth when I say this sound. /**oi**/ [Say a very round /**aw**/ and glide to /**ee**/]

Say the word '**oil**' and listen for the sound /**oi**/. Is it the first or the last sound?

Say the word '**boy**' and listen for the sound /**oi**/. Is it the first or the last sound?

Now listen to these words and raise your hand when you hear the sound /**oi**/. Tell me if it is the first, the middle or the last sound.

| | | | |
|---|---|---|---|
| **toy** | **soil** | **join** | **oil** |
| **coin** | **point** | **voice** | |

I will say the next word slowly. Raise your hand when you hear the sound /**oi**/.

    **r---oy---u---l**

Push the sounds together to make the word.

--------------------------------------------------------------------------------------------

If your child needs extra practice, do more words with /**oi**/. Move ahead to Word Fun.

**the sound /oi/**        **Word Fun**

As a general rule the <u>**oi**</u> spelling comes at the beginning or middle of words, and <u>**oy**</u> comes at the end of a word or a syllable.   You might want to point this out.

**Do the copying and writing exercises.**

# oi

| | | | |
|---|---|---|---|
| **c---oi---n** | **coin** | **s---oi---l** | **soil** |
| b---oi---l | **boil** | b---r---oi---l | **broil** |
| ch---oi---ce | **choice** | j---oi---n | **join** |
| n---oi---se | **noise** | oi---l | **oil** |
| oi---ng---k | **oink** | p---oi---n---t | **point** |
| p---oi---se | **poise** | c---oi---l | **coil** |
| s---p---oi---l | **spoil** | v---oi---ce | **voice** |

# oy

| | | | |
|---|---|---|---|
| **b---oy** | **boy** | **c---oy** | **coy** |
| **j---oy** | **joy** | **t---oy** | **toy** |
| **R---oy** | **Roy** | **s---oy** | **soy** |
| **l---oy---a---l** | **loyal** | **r---oy---a---l** | royal |
| **e---n---j---oy** | **enjoy** | | |

184

# Really Reading
### Reading words with the sound /oi/

## *Joy and Roy*

Joy is shy.
Joy is coy.
Roy is not.
Roy is a boy.

Joy is kind.
She has a coin.
Joy goes to a shop
to get Roy a toy.

Roy is mean.
He is in a club.
He says that Joy can't join.
He says Joy won't enjoy it,
because she's not a boy.

Roy's voice is loud.
He makes lots of noise.
Joy's voice is soft.
Joy has poise.

## the sound /er/    Miss Herd the Nurse

It is advisable to read the Vowel + r section in the Introduction to this Section before you start this set of vowels. These vowels vary greatly by dialect. The pronunciations for /**er**/ range from 'rrrr' to 'uh'. Read the story. Do the listening exercise. Reread the story and play the listening game. Go to Word Fun.

Miss Herd was a nurse.
The best nurse in the world.
If the animals felt bad or worse,
she said, "You'll get well. You have my word."

Miss Herd saw creatures one by one,
over hill and over dale.
She didn't stop til she was done.
It was never too early and never too late.

---

### Listening for the sound /er/

**Read each sentence to your child.**

The sound you hear the most in this story is /**er**/.

Watch my mouth when I say this sound. /**er**/ [Say it in your dialect.]

Now you say the sound /**er**/.

Say the word 'her' and listen for the sound /**er**/. Is it the first or the last sound?

Listen to these words and raise your hand when you hear the sound /**er**/. Then tell me if it is the first, middle, or the last sound.

|        |        |        |
|--------|--------|--------|
| **curl** | **sir** | **earn** |
| **work** | **serve** | **taller** |

I'm going to say the next word slowly. Raise your hand when you hear the sound /**er**/.

**s---p---ea---k---er**

Push the sounds together to make the word.

------------------------------------------------------------------------------------------

If your child needs extra practice, do more words with /**er**/. Reread the story and do the listening game. Then move ahead to Word Fun.
**This is the last listening exercise.**

## the sound /er/          Word Fun

There are five spellings for the sound /er/ in this section. The spelling **er** is by far the most common spelling for this sound. It appears mainly at the ends of multi-syllable words.

# er

| t---er---n | tern | t---i---g---er | tiger |
| t---oa---s---t---er | toaster | m---ow---er | mower |

| e---v---er | **ever** | e---v---er---y | **every** |
| h---er | **her** | h---er---d | **herd** |
| j---er---k | **jerk** | o---v---er | **over** |
| n---er---ve | **nerve** | s---er---ve | **serve** |

## 'per'  words:

| p--er--f—e--c--t | perfect | p--er--s--o--n | person |
| p--er---f---u---m-e | perfume | p--er--m--i--t | permit |

## Make a New Word

Copy these words onto a piece of paper. Have the child write **er** at the end of each word, and read the new word. Spend some time discussing the meaning of these words before and after the **er** is added.

| bank | deep | green | mean |
| cheap | heat | lead | speak |
| calm | small | tall | weak |
| wait | play | kind | bright |
| dark | cold | old | own |

# the sound /er/

# ur

| | | | |
|---|---|---|---|
| **n---ur---se** | **nurse** | **ch---ur---ch** | **church** |
| **t---ur---t---u---l** | **turtle** | **t---ur---k---ey** | **turkey** |
| b---ur---n | **burn** | b---urr | **burr** |
| b---l---ur | **blur** | b---ur---s---t | **burst** |
| c---ur---l | **curl** | c---ur---ve | **curve** |
| f---ur | **fur** | h---urr---y | **hurry** |
| h---ur---t | **hurt** | l---ur---ch | **lurch** |
| p---urr | **purr** | s---l---ur | **slur** |
| t---ur---n | **turn** | ur---ge | **urge** |

**Special word:**       sure
   Say, this is:      shur

# the sound /er/

# ir

| | | | |
|---|---|---|---|
| b---ir---d | **bird** | g---ir---l | **girl** |
| f---ir | **fir** | sh---ir---t | **shirt** |

| | | | |
|---|---|---|---|
| b---ir---ch | **birch** | b---ir---th | **birth** |
| ch---ir---p | **chirp** | d---ir---t | **dirt** |
| f---ir---m | **firm** | f---ir---s---t | **first** |
| s---ir | **sir** | s---qu---ir---m | **squirm** |
| s---qu---ir---t | **squirt** | s---t---ir | **stir** |
| s---w---ir---l | **swirl** | th---ir---d | **third** |
| th---ir---s---t | **thirst** | wh---ir---l | **whirl** |

# the sound /er/

## (w) or

| | | | |
|---|---|---|---|
| w---or---d | word | w---or---k | work |
| w---or---l---d | world | w---or---m | worm |
| w---orr---y | worry | w---or---se | worse |
| w---or---th | worth | | |

Special word:    were

## ear

| | | | |
|---|---|---|---|
| ear---l---y | early | ear---n | earn |
| ear---th | earth | h---ear---d | heard |
| l---ear---n | learn | s---ear---ch | search |

------------------------------------------------------------------------

**ear**    also stands for the sound **/eer/**   **hear** **near**

## Really Reading
## Reading words with the sound /er/

Help with the words    **Merle**,  **squirrel**,  **gurgle**,  **Roger**, **doctor**.

## *Burt the Turtle*

Burt the Turtle sat in the dirt.
He heard a bird and began to search
He saw a bird in a tree.
Sitting next to Merle the squirrel.

The bird gave a chirp.
The squirrel gave a gurgle.
They said, Burt, better scurry.
There's Roger the Tiger.
He will eat you in a hurry.
He'll eat you first.
You'll need a doctor and a nurse.

Burt began to wiggle and squirm.
He took off his tie.
He took off his shirt.
He dug a big hole right in the dirt.

Soon he was under the earth.
He could not be seen.  He could not be heard.

-------------------------------------------------------------------------------
**Do the Word Fun exercise for /ar/.**

## the sound /ar/ Word Fun

How you teach this lesson depends on your dialect. If you pronounce the 'rr' in this vowel then read the first sentence. If you pronounce **ar** as 'ah' in father, read the second sentence.

1. The sound **/ar/** has one main spelling. Lucky for you.

2. This in another way to spell the sound 'ah' like in 'father' and 'grass'.

# ar

| | | | |
|---|---|---|---|
| ar---t | art | c---ar | car |
| f---ar---m | farm | s---t---ar | star |

| | | | |
|---|---|---|---|
| arm | bark | charm | chart |
| cart | carve | dark | far |
| hard | mark | park | part |
| start | starve | tart | yard |
| pardon | | | |

### Special words:

| | | | |
|---|---|---|---|
| ar(e) | are | h---ear---t | heart |
| b---orr---ow | borrow | s---orr---ow | sorrow |
| t---o---m---orr---ow | tomorrow | | |

There is no further exercise or story for this sound. All vowel+r sounds will appear in the last story.

**the sound /or/**          **Off Shore**

Read the story for enjoyment.  Read the story again and play the listening game.
Dialect is important here.  The pronunciation is either **/aw/** or **/oe/-/er/.**  If you
aren't sure about this vowel, read the Introduction to this Section at Vowel+r.


Billy Boar and a warthog named Tor
were born on the shore of Lake Lizzor Lor.
One day, there was a boat by the shore
of Lake Lizzor Lor.
It hadn't been there before.

"Hey Billy, look at that boat.
It has an oar."

"You can't count.  There's more.
I think there are four."

"Two for me," said Billy Boar.
"And two for me," said Warthog Tor.


**Go to Word Fun.**

**the sound /or/**         **Word Fun**

The sound **/or/** has three main spellings: **or** **ore** and **oar**. Do the copying and spelling exercises for each page separately.

# or

| | | | |
|---|---|---|---|
| f---or---k | fork | f---or---t | fort |
| h---or---se | horse | s---t---or---k | stork |
| | | | |
| or | or | f---or | for |
| b---or---n | born | c---or---d | cord |
| c---or---n | corn | f---or---ce | force |
| f---or---m | form | n---or---th | north |
| p---or---ch | porch | p---or---t | port |
| sh---or---t | short | s---or---t | sort |
| s---p---or---t | sport | s---t---or---m | storm |
| t---or---n | torn | w---or---n | worn |

| | |
|---|---|
| f---or---e---s---t | forest |
| or---d---er | order |
| m---or---n---i---ng | morning |

194

# the sound /or/

## ore

| | | | |
|---|---|---|---|
| a---d---ore | **adore** | b---ore | **bore** |
| ch---ore | **chore** | m---ore | **more** |
| s---c---ore | **score** | sh---ore | **shore** |
| s---ore | **sore** | s---t---ore | **store** |
| t---ore | **tore** | w---ore | **wore** |

## oar

| | | | |
|---|---|---|---|
| b---oar | **boar** | b---oar---d | **board** |
| c---oar---se | **coarse** | r---oar | **roar** |
| s---oar | **soar** | | |

## our

| | | | |
|---|---|---|---|
| f---our | **four** | p---our | **pour** |
| s---our—ce | **source** | y---our | **your** |

**Special words:**   **war**   **wart**

**door**   **floor**   **poor**
dor   flor   por

Go to the next page and do the sound **/air/.**

195

**the sound /air/**     **Word Fun**

There is no parent/teacher story for the sound **/air/**. This sound is a glide between **/e/** and **/er/**, or **/eh/—/uh/**, depending on your dialect. **Do the copying and spelling exercises.**

# are

| | | | |
|---|---|---|---|
| b---are | **bare** | b---l---are | **blare** |
| c---are | **care** | d---are | **dare** |
| f---are | **fare** | g---l---are | **glare** |
| h---are | **hare** | p---are | **pare** |
| r---are | **rare** | s---c---are | **scare** |
| sh---are | **share** | s---p---are | **spare** |
| s---qu---are | **square** | s---t---are | **stare** |
| w---are | **ware** | | |

# air

| | | | |
|---|---|---|---|
| air | **air** | ch---air | **chair** |
| f---air | **fair** | h---air | **hair** |
| p---air | **pair** | s---t---air | **stair** |

## the sound /air/

# ear

| | | | |
|---|---|---|---|
| b---ear | **bear** | p---ear | **pear** |
| s---w---ear | **swear** | t---ear | **tear** |
| w---ear | **wear** | | |

# err

| | | | |
|---|---|---|---|
| b---err---y | **berry** | ch---err---y | **cherry** |
| err---or | **error** | t---err---i---b---u---l | **terrible** |

Special words:  **very**      **where**
                    v—air—y     wh---air

**their**       **there**       **they're**

SAY: "These three words all sound alike but mean different things. There are more words like this on the next page."

# The Sound /air/

Here are words that sound alike but mean different things.  These words are
called '**homophones**' – "same-sound."   Go through these words, provide a
definition, and put each word in a sentence.  Ask the child to make a different
sentence for each word.

| | | |
|---|---|---|
| bear | bare | |
| stare | stair | |
| fair | fare | |
| hare | hair | |
| pare | pair | pear |
| wear | ware | where |
| they're | their | there |

## Really Reading
### Mixing vowel+r words

Insist that the child attempt to sound out every word. Help with the words *potatoes, walked, knocked, breakfast, lived, helped*. Define '**ajar**'.

## *Goldilocks and the Three Bears*
### (Revised)

Once upon a time there was a little girl named Goldilocks.
Goldilocks had long, blond, curly hair.
One day she went for a long walk.
She came to a fork in the path, and she forgot which way to go.
She took the wrong turn.
Goldilocks walked on and on, and she got lost.
She was lost in a deep forest of fir and birch trees.

It was nearly dark. The air grew cold and damp.
There was a storm and it started to pour.

Just then, Goldilocks saw a farmyard.
She saw a farmhouse with a porch.
Goldilocks ran to the porch for shelter.
When she got there, the door was ajar.

She knocked on the door, but nobody came.
Nobody was at home, and Goldilocks went inside.
The lights were all on.
There was a blare from a TV.
Goldilocks thought this was very odd.
Who lived here? Where were they?

Then Goldilocks saw a table laid for supper.
There were three plates.
There were three sets of knives, spoons, and forks.
On a sideboard there was steaming, hot food.
The food was keeping warm on hot trays.

There was roast turkey and roast pork.
There were parsnips, turnips, and carrots.
There was mashed potatoes and gravy.
There were fresh pears.
There were berry tarts and cherry tarts.

Goldilocks was starving.
She filled a plate with food.
She went to sit down, but the chairs were strange.
One was very large and too hard.
One was very small.
But one was perfect.
Goldilocks sat down to eat.

She had some turkey and pork.
She had some potatoes with gravy.
She did not have any parsnips, turnips or carrots.
She ate four tarts in all,
two cherry tarts and two berry tarts.
She ate a fresh pear.
She drank a glass of milk.
Goldilocks made a bit of a mess.
There was crust from the tarts all over the floor.

By now, Goldilocks was very full.
She was very tired.
She wanted to go to bed.
There were no beds downstairs.
So Goldilocks went to look upstairs.

She saw three beds, but they were strange too.
One was too hard and too long.
One was too soft and too short.
But one was just perfect.
Goldilocks got in and fell fast asleep.

After a short time, the owners came home.
There was Papa Bear, Mama Bear, and Baby Bear.
They had gone out for a little walk before supper.

Mama Bear saw that the door was ajar.
She said to Papa Bear, "I thought I told you to lock the door,
and turn off that TV."

They came in and shut the door tight.
They took off their raincoats and hung them up to dry.
Mama Bear told Baby Bear to turn off the TV.

Then Mama Bear saw that someone had been there.
First, she saw that some turkey and pork were missing.
Next, she saw that potatoes and gravy were missing.
Then, she saw that four tarts were missing.

She said to Papa Bear,
"Someone has eaten our food."
Then she went over to the table.
She said, "Someone has been sitting in my chair.
Someone has made a mess on the floor."

"My word!" said Papa Bear.
"Who in the world could it be?"
The bears began to worry.

Mama Bear said, "Well whoever it is, they can't be far.
It's too wet and too dark to go out in that storm."
And the weather is getting worse."

Now Baby Bear was afraid.
He said, "You mean someone is still in our house?"
Mama Bear said, "We had better search."

They went upstairs to look around.
Papa Bear went first.

There was no one in Papa Bear's bed.
There was no one in Baby Bear's bed.
But in Mama Bear's bed,
they saw bright yellow curls on the pillow.

Papa Bear said, "Well, well, what have we here?
One little girl with yellow hair.
She came in to get out of the storm.
She must be lost.  She was very hungry and tired."

Papa Bear said, "I'll carry her downstairs,
and put her in my big TV chair."

Then the three bears had their supper and went to bed.

The next morning, Goldilocks got a big surprise.
When she woke up, she saw three pairs of eyes.
She heard three bears say almost at once:
"Good morning," "good morning," "good morning."

Goldilocks was lucky.
The bears were kind and friendly.
Goldilocks said, "Thank you very much for my supper."
Then she helped with the chores.
She swept up her mess on the floor.

Mama Bear made a big breakfast.
After breakfast, the three bears led Goldilocks back to her
home.

Now Goldilocks has three good friends in the forest.

# Where Do You Go From Here?

So far children have learned nearly all the spelling code at the phoneme level, and some of the code at the morpheme level—the smallest sound unit that contains meaning (explained on the next page). The following list identifies what children actually know at this stage.

## Sound Steps Scoreboard

Children have learned:

*All the sounds or phonemes in the English language except one.* The sound **/zh/** is not taught in Sound Steps. It comes in with French and Latin derived words such as vi**si**on (v-i-zh-u-n) and trea**s**ure (t-r-e-zh-ur).

The most common spelling for each of the sounds.

Which sounds have only one main spelling (predictable), regardless of where they come in the word.

Which sounds have predictable spellings by their position in words.

Which sounds have multiple spelling alternatives not always predictable by where they come in a word.

Many useful spelling patterns.
    double letters stand for one sound

    **e** as a 'diacritic'- a mark indicating an altered sound-- for final consonants:
    **ve, se, ce, ze, the, ge, dge**

    common words with irregular spellings that come in small families:
    **break, steak, great // could, should, would // talk, walk, chalk**.

Most high frequency words with truly irregular spellings like: **the of does was**

### What Comes Next?

Children know nearly all parts of the spelling code at the phoneme level. For most, the less common spellings will be learned through increasing exposure to print and formal spelling lessons at school. But, this may not happen, and it is important to monitor children's progress. Listen to them read often. Inspect their written work from school to be sure they are moving ahead correctly.

You can also help by using Sound Steps in a new way. Have children read the Storybook starting with **Poppy Pig**. For each story, follow these instructions to develop this into a spelling exercise. To find out what the child does and doesn't know, consult the Spelling Charts on the next pages. These will show all the spelling alternatives children have been taught, along with words in the story with new spellings.

**Reading Out Loud.**
Ask the child to read the Storybook stories to you. Be sure he tries to read every word. Don't let him paraphrase the story because he knows it already. If the target sound has multiple spellings, and the story is long, break it into two sections and do each section on a different day. Focus your attention on how he reads the words with the target sound. *If he misreads a word containing the target sound,* do one of two things:

If the spelling has already been taught, tell him to segment each sound, blend the sounds into the word, and then say the word again, fluently. **Copy this word onto a spelling list.**

If the spelling has not been taught, point to the new spelling and say the target sound for him. Ask him to segment each sound, blend the sounds into the word, and then say the word again, fluently. **Copy this word onto the spelling list**.

If he misreads a long, difficult word like '**magnificent**' (in *Millicent Mouse*), read the word for him. Next, sound out the syllables: 'mag-ni-fi-cent' and have him imitate you. If he wants the word added to his spelling list as a bonus word, fine. If not, leave it off.

**Copying and spelling from memory**. When you are finished with the story, or story section, have the child copy the words from your list plus the words with new spelling alternatives several times. Next, dictate the words in scrambled order for a spelling test.

## The Morpheme Level of the Spelling Code

A morpheme is the smallest sound unit that contains meaning. A morpheme can be a word or a single letter. Children have already mastered several kinds of morphemes, like the plural, and adding **ing** and **er**. Morphemes added to root words are called prefixes and suffixes: 'happy' plus **un er est** = *un*happy, happi*er*, happi*est*.

As children begin to read and spell words at a more advanced level, certain difficulties may arise. Adding suffixes to English root words can impact how the preceding vowel is pronounced, or how a spelling pattern must alter.

Here are a few examples:

1.  A letter in the root word is changed: *happy    happier*

2.  In suffixes that start with a vowel, this vowel substitutes for the letter **e** in **vowel + e** spellings, acting back on the preceding vowel. *save/saving,    trade/trading,  pine/pined,  craze/crazy.*  It is often necessary to double the consonant to block this 'rule': *bat/batting* (not bating), *cat/catty* (not caty), *ship/shipped* (not shiped).

3.  All past tense verbs end in the letters **ed** even though the pronunciation can be: **/ed/** or **/d/** or **/t/** as in these examples: *decided,  rain'd, walk't.*

4.  Multi-syllable words ending in the sounds /ul/ have multiple spelling alternatives.  Although this spelling is mainly **le** (from the French), it isn't predictable for a particular syllable: **ta*ble*, tri*bal*, la*bel*, sym*bol*,** nor from one syllable to another: **mar*vel*, na*val*** (and never mar*vle or* na*vle*).

Latin derived words create another set of problems.  Latin words often consist of prefix+root+suffix.  They constitute about 60% of the words in an adult's vocabulary.  Prefixes and roots are spelled predictably, but the suffixes are not.  Here, the spelling maps to the entire suffix (the morpheme).  Because of this, the simplest way to learn these suffixes is by mastering multi-sound 'phonograms'.

For example, there are seven spellings for the suffix '**shun**' and this isn't one of them.  'shun' turns the word into a noun.  **tion** is by far the most common spelling, and used in thousands of words: *information, nation, investigation;* **sion** is the second most common spelling and is mainly governed by the root word ending: *aggress/aggression    express/expression;* **cian** is for an occupation or person: *musician electrician statistician.*  The remaining four spellings are rare.  These are **tian** (dietician), **cion** *suspicion,* **cean** *ocean,* and **shion**, *cushion.*

There are about 20 Latin suffixes with multiple spelling alternatives.  They can be mastered by taking advantage of these patterns and their frequency in the language.  Words derived from the Greek have special spellings to mark them out as "Greek," such as using the letter **y** to stand for the sound /i/ as in *symbol, myth, mystery, sympathy.*

**The advanced levels of the spelling code are taught in Allographs II (Trafford Publishers) and available on Trafford.com.**

# Scoreboard for Spelling Alternatives Taught

## Consonants

| sound<br>taught | spelling alternatives<br>taught | spelling alternatives<br>not taught |
|---|---|---|
| b | b | -- |
| c (/k/) | c  k  ck | ch  que |
| d | d | -- |
| f | f  ph | gh |
| g | g | gh  gu  gue |
| h | h  wh | -- |
| j | j  ge  dge | g(i)   g(y) |
| l | l | -- |
| m | m | mn  mb |
| n | n  kn  gn | -- |
| p | p | -- |
| qu | qu | -- |
| r | r  wr | -- |
| s | s  se  ce  c | sc |
| t | t | -- |
| v | v  ve | -- |
| w | w  wh | -- |
| x | x | -- |
| z | z  ze  se  s | -- |
| ch | ch  tch | -- |
| ng | ng  n | -- |
| sh | sh | (Latin suffixes) |
| th | th  the | -- |

# Scoreboard for Spelling Alternatives Taught

## Vowels

| sound | spelling alternatives taught | spelling alternatives not taught |
|-------|------------------------------|----------------------------------|
| a | a | -- |
| e | e  ea  ai | -- |
| i | i | y  ui |
| o | a(l)  (w)a | -- |
| u | u  o | ou |
| | | |
| aw | aw  au  ough  augh | -- |
| | | |
| ae | a-e  a  ay  ea  eigh | ei  ey |
| ee | ee  ea  y  e  ey | ie/ei  e-e  i-e  i |
| ie | i-e  i  y  igh | -- |
| oe | o-e  o  oa  ow | -- |
| ue | u-e  u  ew | -- |
| | | |
| oo | oo  u  ou | -- |
| <u>oo</u> | oo  ue  ew  ui | u   ou |
| oi | oi  oy | -- |
| ou | ou  ow | ough |
| | | |
| er | er  ur  ir  (w)or  ear | -- |
| or | or  ore  oar  our  oor | -- |
| air | air  are  err  ear | arr |

# Storybook Score Card

## Spellings from the Storybook Taught and Not Taught in the Lessons

## *SECTION I*

| Story | Spellings Taught | | | Spellings Not Taught |
|---|---|---|---|---|
| **Poppy Pig** | **p** | **pp** | | |
| **Timmy Tuttle** | **t** | **tt** | | |
| **The Loch Ness Monster** | **o** | **(w)a** | | **gone**<br>**ough** (thought) |
| **Mr. & Mrs. Mouse**<br>**Mr. Mrs.** | **m** | **mm** | | **mn** (column)<br>**mb** (climb) |
| **Ned Learns** | **n** | **nn** | **kn** | |
| **Ann's Hat** | **a** | | | |
| **Last Dinosaur** | **d** | **dd** | | |
| **Six Witches** | **i** | | | **y** (hymn) |
| **Greg's Goat** | **g** | **gg** | | |
| **Billy** | **b** | **bb** | | |
| **Uttley** | **u** | **o** | | **ou**<br>(young)<br>(touch)<br>(country) |
| **Leonard Leopard** | **e** | **ea** | **ai** | **Leonard, leopard** |

# Storybook Score Card

## *SECTION II*

| Story | Spellings Taught | Spellings Not Taught/Irreg. |
|---|---|---|
| **Harper** | h<br>w   wh | |
| **The Rescue** | r   wr | |
| **Just July** | j   ge   dge | **g (**before <u>e</u>, i  <u>y</u>)<br>giant<br>gorgeous<br>gentle<br>gym |
| **Driving Lesson** | v   ve<br>z   zz  s  ze  se | |
| **Yellow Balloon** | l   ll   le (/ul/) | |
| **Fox and the Wolf** | f   ff   ph | **gh**<br>rough<br>enough |
| **Sam's Escape** | c  s  ss  ce  se | **c** (y)   **sc**<br>cycled   scene |

# Storybook Score Card

## SECTION III

| Story | Spellings Taught | | | Spellings Not Taught/Irreg. | | |
|---|---|---|---|---|---|---|
| **King Karl** | **k** | **c** | **ck** | | | |
| | **qu** (kw) | | | | | |
| | **x** (ks) | | | | | |
| **Silver Shadow** | **sh** | | | **ce**an | ocean | |
| | | | | **ti**on | invention | |
| | | | | **ci**al | special | |
| **The Pudding** | **oo** | **u** | **ou(l)** | | | |
| **The New Sign** | **oo** | **ue** | **ew** | **o** | who | move |
| | | | | **ough** | through | |
| **Queen Beth** | **th** | **the** | | | | |
| **King Ching** | **ng** | **n(k)** | | | | |
| **Water Witch** | **ch** | **tch** | | | | |

# Storybook Score Card

## *SECTION IV*

| Story | Spellings Taught | Spellings Not Taught |
|---|---|---|
| **Mean Dragon** | ee    ea    e    y | **ie**    **e-e**    **i** |
| | | fierce    Zeke    safari |
| | | fiend     scheme |
| | | stories   serene |
| | | niece     scene |
| | | field |
| | | relief |
| **Austin Auk** | aw    au    ough    augh | |
| **Abe the Ape** | a-e    ai    ay    a    eigh    ea | Hey |
| **Nigel the Nice** | i-e    ie    i    y    igh | |
| **Mole's Biznis** | o-e    oe    o    oa    ow | |
| **O.U. Mule** | u-e    ue    u    ew | **eau** (beautiful) |
| **Olly Owl** | ou    ow | **ough** (bough) |
| **Roy's Noise** | oi    oy | |
| **Miss Herd** | er    ur    ir    or    ear | |
| **Off Shore** | or    ore    oar    our    (w)ar | |

211

Printed in the United States
By Bookmasters